MW01064807

SEAN

The Story of a Child's Life and Death

by
Julie Maude Miller

Dry Bones Press
San Francisco, California

Sean

The Story of a Child's Life & Death

by Julie Maude Miller

Publisher
Dry Bones Press, Inc.
P. O. Box 640345
San Francisco, CA 94164
(415) 707–2129
http://www.drybones.com/

Publisher's Cataloging–in–Publication
Miller, Julie M. (Julie Maude), 1958—
    SEAN: The Story of a Child's Life and
    Death / Julie Maude Miller
    p.   c.
    ISBN 1–883938–39–2
1. Carcinoma 2. Chemotherapy 3. Oncology
4. Cancer—Treatment 5. Patients—Psychology
6. Death and dying.
I. Title II. Author.
RC280   616.9'99

Sean

SEAN

Before you cross the street
take my hand
Life is what happens to you
while you're busy making other plans

Beautiful
Beautiful beautiful
Beautiful boy
Darling
Darling Sean

Beautiful Boy
by John Lennon

BEAUTIFUL BOY

Many families have lost a child to cancer, and everyone has a unique insight. This is mine, a year-long journal I kept after the death of our 14 year old son. Sean was born on a rainy Easter Sunday morning in 1981, a gentle and undemanding child who shared the name of John Lennon's youngest son, for whom the songwriter wrote the song, *Beautiful Boy.* We listened to that particular Lennon tune the night Sean was dying and played it again at his funeral. The lyrics are touching, the music enchanting and sweet, and the message of the lullaby one we wanted to convey.

Sean will always be our beautiful boy.

I wrote this book for three reasons. First, I felt compelled to, because countless families endure a loss like ours each year, and I strongly believed a current, first-hand account should exist. It is the only kind of narrative that accurately reflects what happens to families when a child dies, and what cancer treatment for children is like in the late twentieth century.

Secondly, I believed that anyone who had ever loved could benefit from reading Sean's story. It is detailed and real; there is no sugar-coating, only honesty, and you do not have to be the parent of a dying child to understand our experiences. Anyone who has cared for children or lost someone close, can relate to this story of love.

Finally, I underwent a spiritual evolution during Sean's illness, and especially after his death. I am not a particularly religious person, so the spiritual experiences were somewhat of a surprise. I know now that many people have had similar encounters, and for those who have not, perhaps my account can give them some measure of hope in what has become an increasingly hopeless world. I believe my son's spirit lives on, and that wherever he is, he is not alone. Everyone who has been lost to this world, is with him.

My daughter, Hayley, wrote about her brother a year after he died. She was eight years old at the time and had written the narrative one day at school. We had worried that Hayley would not remember her brother or his illness because she was only seven when he died, but our fears were unfounded. Her simple essay illustrates the profound impact a child's death has on everyone in the family.

"MY BROTHER"

by Hayley Miller

I have a brother. His name is Sean. When he started hurting all over his body, we discovered that he had cancer. My family was very disappointed. The cancer was called Rhabdomyosarcoma. It was stage four and that is really bad. When his hair started falling out, we had to shave his head. First it scared my mom, but she got used to it.

Sean threw up almost every day. He was rather nice to me. He had to go to the Salt Lake hospital for a bone marrow transplant. He got sicker and looked different. He took naps a lot. After the bone marrow transplant, the cancer didn't come back. But then one day it came back. Sean was really mad, because every day he would feel terrible. I played games with him sometimes, but often he was too sick to play.

After a few months he died upstairs on the couch. It grew sadness in our family.

We had a very nice funeral for him. He was fourteen and battled cancer for two years.

Sean will always be in my heart.

SEAN

Sean, with Hayley & Tyler

"Sean was here—"

AUGUST

When you are joyous, look deep into your heart
and you shall find it is only that which has
given you sorrow that is giving you joy.

When you are sorrowful look again in your heart,
and you shall see that in truth you are weeping for
that which has been your delight.

Some of you say, "Joy is greater than sorrow," and
others say, "Nay, sorrow is the greater." But I say
unto you, they are inseparable.

Together they come, and when one sits alone with
you at your board, remember that the other is
asleep upon your bed.

"On Joy and Sorrow"

—Kahlil Gibran, *The Prophet*

August 10, 1995

Sean has been dead for a week. He was fourteen years old. His funeral was three days ago, and all the family and visitors are gone. Now I know what it means to have a broken heart. My heart hurts, literally. I didn't know that grief was a physical condition as well as an emotional burden. The pain is palpable, and the deep sadness an integral part of me. I cannot imagine feeling happy again, or believing that life is promising and holds some measure of magic. Peace is the most I can hope for, and that seems far into the future.

The hurt is constant, but I am moving through the routine of everyday life, pretending I am strong and that I will be all right. Sometimes I pretend I'm the person I used to be when Sean was alive, and I could live for the joy of that day because although he had cancer, he was still alive! Then I remember he is gone, and I can't find him in his bed or on the sofa, and I cry. The grief in this house is so thick, you would need a machete to cut your way through it.

I didn't cry at the funeral, and was able to accompany my nephew on the piano as he sang "Fire and Rain" by James Taylor. I went through the motions without a breakdown; my reserve was intact. I wonder if I should pat myself on the back. I wonder if Sean thinks I didn't care enough to cry.

We dressed him in blue and white Duke basketball shorts over silk boxers, his Harley Davidson scarf, and a

SEAN

NO FEAR T-shirt, because that describes how Sean approached his life and death. The back of the T-shirt read, *Live free - - or die.* It wasn't exactly Sean's choice, but that is what happened. My childhood friend, Melody was at the funeral with her family, and her husband built Sean's pine casket, lining it with soft plaid flannel. He had offered to do it a few weeks before Sean died, worried that I would be offended by the suggestion, but I was not. I was moved to tears that he would do something so wonderful for us and for our dying son.

Sean's name was engraved on the top, but the funeral director covered the engraving with the spray of wildflowers we had carefully chosen. I stood up as they moved by, wheeling the casket, and asked them to move the flowers so we could see Sean's name. Afterwards, Melody said, with a hint of a smile, because we try to make life into one big, bad joke whenever we are together: "When I saw you do that, I knew you had things under control, Julie."

I am sure it appeared that way, because that was my intent. I wanted to be dignified like Sean was when he lost his hair, his friends, a right testicle, and the control of his bladder when new tumors lodged near his kidney. After the initial diagnosis, when we told our twelve year old son he had Stage IV cancer and explained what that meant, Sean was lying in a Salt Lake City hospital bed, weakened and nauseated. "Oh, so that's what it is," he said softly. There were no tears, no "Why me's??" - just simple acceptance and dignity.

In retrospect, maintaining a wooden composure at my beloved son's funeral service does not seem dignified; it seems rather unnatural. Why couldn't I cry? What was I trying to prove? Sometimes I wish I had fallen apart and made a spectacle of myself so people would not expect anything from me.

Controlling my tears, however, has become a habit. I held them in during Sean's illness because he couldn't cope with emotional displays, especially from me. Whenever I did break down, he would hold his hand up and say, quietly but firmly, "Mom, don't cry. Please." I understand why he depended on our strength, though it was only skin-deep. He didn't need to watch his parents fall apart as he struggled with the devastating changes in his life and the possibility of no future here with us.

But now it feels as if a dam has burst and I cannot control it. The tears keep flowing. I think about our dead son most of my waking hours and many of the hours I'm supposed to be sleeping, because that is the worst time. When night closes in, so does life, and there is nothing left to distract me. I imagine Sean's voice when I open the front door. "Mom, come upstairs. Where have you been?" He always demanded a strict accounting of my comings and goings.

Sometimes I see him too, thin and gaunt, but smiling happily as we went out to lunch or to the mall. He loved going out with his family, but whenever we planned a small excursion an undercurrent of tension accompanied us, as if we knew something would happen to take it away. It often did. Several times, after we had arrived at a restaurant for lunch, Sean would get a bloody nose and we would have to leave. He would hold a tissue up to his nose, desperately trying to stop the bleeding, but it usually continued until we had returned home. We didn't give up trying to find things he could enjoy, but Sean had to work for every bit of pleasure. Nothing was given to him without a catch. I remember watching him hobble around at the county fair last year (after the bone marrow transplant) with his best friend, Casey. Sean was determined to enjoy himself, though his physical body refused to cooperate. His body, not his spirit, betrayed

13

him.

I try to understand the spiritual aspects of his death, and I want to believe that he is happy and free of the limitations of his physical body, perhaps living in another world, another dimension. I feel him with me constantly, so I cannot accept the notion that death means annihilation. But I have no quarrel with those who do. It is difficult to imagine something wonderful emerging from all this misery. I like the following quote from the 1994 film *The Shawshank Redemption* about hope. "Hope is a good thing, maybe the best of things, and no good thing ever dies." That explains how I feel about Sean, our middle child, who was born on Easter Sunday over fourteen years ago.

No one understands me like he did, and I am afraid I will never love anyone in quite the same way. I love our two surviving children and my husband deeply, but it was different with Sean. He seemed like part of me, and that is why I feel half formed, incomplete. I want to be with him again and see his smile, change the dressings on his broviac catheter, help him with his bath, fix his meals, and take in all that was good and wonderful surrounding him. After Sean was diagnosed with Stage IV cancer in October of 1993, our roles gradually reversed without my knowledge. He became the parent who quietly taught me how to live, and I became the child who scarcely knew what she was learning until the teacher had gone.

Did Sean know he was going to die before it happened? He was a cheerful, optimistic child and wanted everyone around him to be happy. But during the brief remission of four or five months, after the initial rounds of intensive chemotherapy and radiation followed by a bone marrow transplant, he wrote a poem at school about having cancer. The melancholy and doom in his writing was uncharacteristic of Sean. Maybe he considered poetry a safe expression of what he knew was going to happen, a warning to the rest of us perhaps, though we didn't see it that way at the time.

The poem was read at his funeral and printed in a collection of student poetry circulated at the junior high school he attended.

"THE CANCER IS THERE"

The Cancer is there
No one can compare
Your new life has begun
and it's not going to be fun
Your life will continue
even though it's new
The Cancer is there

You are going to get drugs
but it will kill the bugs
You will get sick
but it will go away quick
You will get a shot
but it will be forgot
The Cancer is there

Now you are worried
because you are hurried
The doc lies you down
and you put on a gown
They do some tests
but it's for the best
The Cancer is gone

4 months go by

15

SEAN

and you think you won't die
Then you get sick
It hits you like a brick
They do some more tests
Now you must rest
The Cancer is there

They put you in bed
and now you dread
the things that come
You now feel numb
You think you will die
Oh why Oh why

Now you are dead
Alone ... in your bed
The Cancer is dead.

—Sean Miller

August 12, 1995

We left town yesterday. The emptiness at home had become overwhelming and we needed to escape, if only for a day. We drove to Boise, stayed over night in a hotel, and did some school shopping for Hayley, our seven-year-old, the only child left at home. The room was upgraded at no charge, and we ended up with a suite, complete with two televisions, a kitchen, microwave, and fridge. Sean

16

would have loved it.

The last time I took him to Primary Children's Hospital in Salt Lake City, when they did a CT scan of his head to determine if the growing bumps were actually tumors, we stayed in a cheap, shabby motel. Sean's happiness was my first consideration, and most of the time we stayed in comfortable hotels for his sake, but that particular time I was trying to save money. It seems incredibly silly now.

The room was clean and neat, but it was not the Marriot, which Sean deserved. I walked through Temple Square and to Crossroads Mall to get us something to eat while Sean laid in bed and watched television. The three and a half hour drive had exhausted him, as usual. When I returned, he said, "This room is just as good as the Marriot, Mom. This is really nice."

He was lying, of course, but it was so sweet. He was trying to make me feel better. I regret not indulging him with a posh hotel room on the final trip to Salt Lake, but I didn't know it would be the last time I would have the opportunity. The tumors mushroomed in the following days, ignoring the last attempts at chemotherapy and destroying our future.

Early this morning, we left Boise and drove east into the mountains, stopping in Idaho City, Lowman, and Stanley. Al, Sean's dad, and I wanted to see the wilderness and take the long way home. We stayed a couple of hours at Redfish Lake in the Sawtooth mountain range, staring into the black water and watching our little girl play in the sand, forcing smiles for her sake. Hayley seemed to enjoy herself, though Al and I were sort of stunned, as if it hadn't sunk in yet but was finally beginning to. We drove on to Ketchum, our childhood home, and ate dinner at the family's favorite Italian restaurant. In between bites of the suddenly tasteless spaghetti and pizza, I cried. Sean would have loved this little trip. He loved going out to dinner with us. Everything has been spoiled. I can't enjoy anything now, because Sean is gone.

August 18, 1995

We received a letter a week ago from one of Sean's best loved doctors in Salt Lake City, Dr. O'Brien. It was dated August 7, the day of Sean's funeral. I was grateful he responded to the news of Sean's death, because I have reached the point where I don't expect anything from people. Somehow, I know they cannot help me. But this letter is much appreciated, and so are the sympathy cards. I didn't know that receiving a simple card could have such a positive impact, but it does. People have no idea how much the little things count until they are vulnerable and suddenly on the receiving end of kindness.

When Sean was undergoing treatment, Dr. O'Brien complimented us on treating him normally, which he believed was the best thing parents could do for a sick kid. I am glad we didn't coddle Sean, because overprotecting him would not have extended his life. It would have made him a sad and lonely boy. As far as behavior was concerned, we did demand a certain level of conformity, but when he was too sick to bear up, we backed off. Sean rarely took advantage, but sometimes I feel guilty about requiring the same behavior from him as I did from our other kids. His life was different from theirs.

I have saved a poignant letter from Casey, Sean's best friend. Casey was a year older, and before Sean got cancer, they were casual friends and close neighbors. But after Sean's diagnosis, they became *best* friends, and Casey never let Sean down. How many kids do you know who become best friends with someone who has cancer? Almost none, I would venture to say. It is just too frightening. Casey watched Sean throw up and lay on the couch, too weak and tired to do anything but watch television, but he continued to visit nearly every day. He allowed Sean to lay down the ground rules for what they did together. A few weeks ago Casey said, "I don't think other kids realize that for Sean, a trip into town means spending a few minutes at the video store. That's all he can handle."

I recall one night when Casey, Sean, and another friend returned to our house after having dinner at a fast food restaurant. Sean vomited as soon as he got out of the car. Instead of running away and acting afraid, they followed Sean inside and stayed until he asked them to leave. Their courageous behavior showed our son that no matter how bad things became, they were not going to abandon him.

Casey and Sean shared an optimistic outlook for the future and believed Sean would get well. But Casey finally had to face the truth, as we all did, and it must have been terrifying. No matter how difficult it was to watch his friend die, though, this young man kept coming back day after day, even when Sean acted like he didn't want him there.

After Casey found out Sean was definitely dying, Sean became cold and distant towards him. Troubled and sad, Casey came to see me privately a couple of weeks before Sean's death. "What should I do?" he asked soberly, his eyes welling up with tears. "Sean acts like he doesn't want me around. I want to be with him, but only if he wants me there. Just tell me what to do. Please."

19

SEAN

Although I didn't know Sean's true feelings, I had a few ideas. I explained that he was angry and might be testing Casey's love. I also wondered if Sean didn't want anyone to watch him die, because things were getting pretty grisly. Sean could no longer leave the house because the pain in his spinal column was intense whenever he stood up (the bones were deteriorating because of the cancer). He was too nauseated to eat, and when there was no food in his stomach to throw up, he had dry heaves. The tumors on the back of his head were growing rapidly and with a bald head, were clearly visible. He was too tired to play video games and the television irritated him. He was losing bladder control; his abdomen was swelling and causing him constant pain. We were having difficulty finding the right medications to control the pain and he was always uncomfortable.

It could not be hidden from Casey any longer. Sean was dying. We were down to the bad stuff, and all the good stuff was in the past. Sean had always tried to protect Casey from the worst part of his illness, because he wanted them to have fun together as much as possible. He wanted Casey to be a part of his "normal" life, but that was no longer possible.

"I think you need to keep coming," I finally offered. "If you stay away, it will break Sean's heart."

I approached Sean that night, gently but persuasively. "Casey loves you deeply," I pointed out. "He has been through all of this with you, and he still needs your love." I didn't say anything else, but the following morning Sean sought me out.

"I think Casey should come over every day, for a little while," he suggested.

"Would that be good for you?" I asked, suddenly wondering if I had pushed too far and Sean was responding to my pressure rather than his own needs.

"I think it would be good for Casey," he said thoughtfully.

Tyler, our oldest son, thinks we should get down on our knees and thank Casey for being Sean's friend, because what would our boy have done without him? He had other friends, but most of them were uncomfortable with his diagnosis and afraid of what was happening. It was natural to feel that way, and Sean understood. He also knew that at times he was not a lot of fun to be around, but this didn't deter Casey, who was strangely mature and unfailingly loyal. He wrote the following letter in December of 1994, when Sean was in the Utah hospital after the cancer returned, five months after the bone marrow transplant.

Dear Sean,

How is it going? Well, I am sitting in speech with nothing to do, and since I miss you so much, I figured I would write you a letter. It's tough with you not around. You are the only guy I can say anything to and you will listen. I have friends, but you are my only true friend. I wish I were with you always. You really bring out the best in me.

You are a real fighter, Sean. I wish I had the heart and strength you do. I miss all the basketball games we played in the driveway. Those were fun, weren't they? Hell, I don't know why I'm writing this letter. I guess I miss you more than I have ever missed anyone. I know you will get better, but the time in between the before and after is eating away at me. I wish you wouldn't have gotten sick, but I guess life is a bunch of bullshit thrown in one big hole.

SEAN

You are a great pal. I admire you more than anyone else in my life. You are my hero, and I wish I could be more like you. Every time I see you, a smile comes to my face. I wish I could take away the pain and the cancer, but I can't. My prayers, my love, and especially my friendship will always be with you. If you ever need to talk or cry, please call me. I will always be there for you, and I know you will always be there for me.

Love, Casey

Maybe this is what life is all about. Learning how to love and learning how to deal with deep and painful loss. Perhaps this letter sums it all up.

August 20, 1995

The evening following Sean's death, Casey telephoned and asked if he could come over. It was Friday night, so we ordered pizza and watched a video, typical weekend fare for the Miller family. Al, Tyler, Hayley, Casey, and I were doing what we had always done when Sean was with us. It was a familiar ritual. I sat on the sofa where Sean had died, and I felt his presence. I don't know how to explain it, but he was there. A strong physical sensation, an intense burning, permeated my chest. Was it Sean? Was he with us? The feelings were confusing and overwhelming. I suddenly sprang from the sofa and hurried downstairs. I still haven't shared the experience with anyone.

The same thing happened the night he died, after they had taken his cold, still body away. I felt Sean's spirit, not beside me, but *in* me. It was amazing. I could not see him, but was he there?

Holly, Sean's 26 year old English teacher and close friend, shared something with me two days after Sean's death. She and Kelly, another young teacher friend, stopped by the house, and we sat outside on the deck and talked about Sean.

"I want to tell you something," Holly offered tentatively, "but I won't be telling many more people, because I get the *strangest* looks." She laughed and related what had happened on Thursday evening, the night Sean died.

"I went to bed early, about 10:15. I didn't think I could sleep because I was upset about Sean, but miraculously, I drifted off right away. Moby, my big white dog, was sleeping in the bedroom with me. Suddenly, I was awakened by Moby's barking. He was racing around the room in circles, yelping and carrying on, something he had never done before. I was really irritated, because I was dreaming about Sean and didn't want to be interrupted, so I threw a shoe at Moby, hoping to go back to sleep and resume the dream. I looked at the digital clock, and it was 10:45 p.m."

Sean died at 10:40 that night. Did Moby sense someone else was in the room? Holly didn't share her interpretation of what happened, but I think we both know what it meant.

SEAN

August 26, 1995

Al and I have already chosen the headstone. We decided to get it done right away, knowing what we wanted. Sean wouldn't like anything ostentatious, so it is a small, gray stone upright, which will be placed at the head of his grave, with the name Sean Eugene Miller, his date of birth and death, and an etching of a dove at the top. Sean is buried next to his paternal grandfather, Eugene Miller, who also died of cancer shortly after Sean was diagnosed. I have had trouble thinking of a suitable epitaph for the other side, and I have asked for help from our lost son, hoping he can come up with something and plant it in my uninspired mind. Most inscriptions are sappy, and Sean hated the overly sentimental, as I do, so I have been at a loss. I don't want anything reeking of false spirituality either, because I despise pretentiousness.

But today, after a fruitless search through books of quotations and epitaphs, it came to me. Wide eyed, I turned to Hayley and announced, "I know what Sean wants on his headstone. He wants it to read *'Sean was here'*."

When I tried to explain what that meant, I had visions of kids writing graffiti on bathroom walls, that so and so was here, and I could not understand why I thought that should be on our son's memorial marker. Sean wouldn't want something people scribbled on bathroom walls, often mixed in with obscenities, written on his headstone. Maybe I had dreamed it all up, I thought dejectedly.

"But Mom," Hayley said with excitement, "that was in *The Shawshank Redemption*. Remember when they wrote that in the movie?"

A light flickered in my brain, and I knew this was Sean's wish. In the film, there are two separate scenes in which a pair of prison friends are finally parolled, after decades of imprisonment. They stay in a halfway house (in the same room, at different times) while struggling to adjust to an outside world that no longer wants them. Before leaving, they carve the words "Brooks was here" and "So was Red" (respectively), on the wall of their room in the halfway house. Brooks, an elderly and suddenly friendless man, commits suicide. The other man, played by the actor Morgan Freeman, joins another pal who had escaped from prison some time before. It is a touching film about love and friendship and how to maintain them in a desolate world. I know my boy wants the inscription *"Sean was here"* written on his headstone, though people will probably be confused by what it means.

I feel relieved and more connected to my angel son.

August 28, 1995

Today was the first day of school, and I felt sad. Hayley was going and Sean was not. Neither was I, since I had taken an indefinite leave of absence from my teaching job when Sean got sick two years ago. Tyler is at the Air Force Academy in Colorado, where he is a freshman this year, Hayley is starting second grade, and our family seems too small. Things have changed and they are never going to be the same again. My life has been ripped apart. I want to take care of Sean and nothing else seems remotely appealing. I would give anything to have him back, even in moderate health.

I wonder if he would want that, though. The illness was getting very old, the disappointment unending. The summer following Sean's diagnosis was spent in Primary Children's Hospital in Salt Lake City, where he endured the horrors of a bone marrow transplant. For weeks, everything that came out of his body was bloody: emesis, urine, bowel contents. His entire GI tract was raw from intensive chemotherapy, and when he swallowed, he suffered excruciating pain. The morphine pump was supposed to manage the anguish, but the side effects of morphine include nausea and vomiting, so Sean would throw up and his throat would hurt even more. We felt helpless.

When we were with him in the bone marrow transplant unit (for 12 to 16 hours a day), we usually stood at his bedside, because he continually needed the plastic basin to vomit in, a cool washcloth for his feverish forehead, or the suction instrument for the severe mucousitis he was battling. This year, Sean was excited to be spending the summer at home so he could hang out with Casey and have fun, though he was still undergoing chemotherapy after the cancer had returned in November of 1994.

Instead, he got to spend the summer dying.

August 29, 1995

My school teacher friend, Tris (who was also Sean's kindergarten teacher), called to see how I was doing, though she already knows, I think.

"Julie," she offered sadly, "I see Sean everywhere. When I'm out shopping or driving, I see a young boy walking by and I think it is Sean."

The other day I reread the sympathy card Tris sent

when Sean died, and I saw it with new eyes, as I see most things now. It's a watercolor painting of an angel with oversized wings and pale pink swaddling clothes. She is suspended from the sky with a halo of clouds surrounding her, and she is holding a little boy, cradling him in her arms as he sleeps. I hope someone is doing that for Sean. Since it can't be me, I hope someone else is caring for him and making him feel safe and warm and loved.

But I cannot imagine anyone loving him as much as I do.

I was talking on the telephone to my sister-in-law, who has lost three babies, an almost unspeakable tragedy in these modern times, and I told her about this divine card, sharing my hope that someone is encircling our boy with loving, protective arms. She said it was probably Sean who was holding *me* tight, offering comfort because he knew he was the only one who could do it. I framed the card, and it is sitting on my desk, so I can look at it daily and nurture the hope that someone is caring for my beautiful boy. I often think about what my sister in law said, that perhaps Sean's arms are holding me tight, that his spirit burns through my own, and that he continually tries to make his presence and love known to me.

We played a song we love on the stereo the night he was dying, and at the funeral as well, the song that always reminded us of Sean long before he got sick: *"Beautiful Boy"*, by John Lennon. "Darling, darling Sean" are the final words in the song, and I say that to myself each day, in a desperate attempt to find some comfort.

SEAN

August 30, 1995

The mother of one of Sean's childhood friends shared something that cheered me up. His friend, Hailey, was talking about his death with her mom, Kyle, who said, "It's all very sad. Sean is missing out on so much, like graduating from high school and having a first kiss."

"He already had his first kiss," Hailey offered with a sly smile.

"Who was it?" Kyle asked in surprise.

"Me. I kissed Sean at the 6th grade Halloween party we had at our house a couple of years ago."

In ordinary circumstances, I might have thought Sean was too young for a first kiss, but now, you cannot imagine how happy that makes me.

SEPTEMBER

SEAN

Grief fills the room up of my absent child,
Lies in his bed, walks up and down with me,
Puts on his pretty looks, repeats his words,
Remembers me of all his gracious parts,
Stuffs out his vacant garments with his form.

—William Shakespeare

September 7, 1995

I miss Sean's dry sense of humor, which developed after he got sick. His dad is electronics illiterate, and Sean got a kick out of that. Al cannot operate the VCR, and remote controls (when he can find them) baffle him.

"Dad, we're bored," Sean would announce with a mischievous twinkle in his eye. "Let's watch you use the remote." He had a lengthy repertoire of one-liners.

After O.J. Simpson was accused of killing his wife, Sean watched the news update every day and followed the trial. When Al returned home each night, he would ask Sean for an update on O.J. "O.J. is lookin' scared," Sean invariably answered, "he's lookin' *real* scared." Then he would flash a radiant grin, knowing he had made his dad's day.

After Sean got sick, we laid everything out on the table. We no longer avoided discussing personal matters, feeling a strong sense of guilt and responsibility that we hadn't warned the boys to watch their testicles for changes. If we had, maybe our shy and private son would have come to us sooner. The tumor had probably been growing in Sean's right testicle for months; he may have noticed it was larger than the other one, but he kept it to himself. A week or two before the diagnosis of cancer, a hydrocele (a water filled sac) formed around the testicle and swelled to the size of a grapefruit. By then, Sean must have known his right testicle was abnormally large, but he said nothing. Maybe he was too embarrassed to talk about it, or maybe he felt the abnormality was a poor reflection of his developing manhood. The doctor finally discovered the hydrocele during an examination, when he was trying to find an explanation for Sean's constant vomiting and rapid weight loss.

Sean never told us why he felt unable to share this personal information with his parents, and we didn't ask. The subject caused him considerable stress, and every doctor he talked to asked him when the hydrocele had appeared. Sean always claimed that he didn't know, and by then, it was too late for the information to do us any good. With Sean, you had to learn to let things go, because he withdrew when pushed into sharing private matters. Any revelations had to be offered on his own terms.

After Sean got cancer, scores of doctors looked at his tumorous testicle, and that was just the beginning. His body suddenly belonged to medical personnel. The modesty had to be discarded. It was a luxury we could no longer afford. We began talking more openly, making jokes and treating most things with a great deal of irreverence. It made our two boys pretty crass, I admit, but there was no alternative. Our new broadmindedness helped Sean endure the humiliation of being poked at and examined by strangers.

Sean and I visited his pediatrician, Dr. Adrian, often for lab work, checkups, and easily administered chemotherapy like Vincristine in between the trips to the Salt Lake City hospital. We made the best of it while concentrating on the comic aspects of our situation, like dire warnings from dieticians to carefully wash our fruits and vegetables because of pesticides. Toxic chemicals were being poured into Sean's system, and we were supposed to worry about pesticides? That was good for a chuckle or two.

During one visit, Sean and I were giggling and

making fun of things as Dr. Adrian eyed us curiously. "Well," he finally commented, "I suppose it's best to look on the bright side." For us, it helped.

"As long as Sean is laughing and getting some pleasure out of life," Al often said, "we are not quitting on him." Eventually, all the laughing stopped, of course, but not until the end.

Sean was an optimistic, upbeat child, though there were many times when putting on a bright face wasn't possible. When we stayed in Salt Lake City during the initial diagnosis, Al and I took turns sleeping in the hospital room at night because Sean was frightened, and so were we. We never slept well at the hospital because as soon as you drifted off to sleep, a monitor beeped or a nurse popped in and you had to start all over again. Late one night, Sean and I were talking in the darkened room.

"So, is this all my fault?" he asked shakily. I knew he was referring to keeping the changes in his testicle a secret.

I choked back tears and said, "No, of course not. This is nobody's fault."

Then he asked a more difficult question, the only time he voiced the dreaded possibility until the final days of his life. "Mom, am I going to die?"

I paused before replying, "We are going to do everything we can to make sure that doesn't happen." It was a cowardly answer, but all I was capable of. My response told him nothing, except that I did not want to talk about him dying. Maybe I shut him off early on. The oncologists said that young cancer patients try to protect their parents, but I thought our kids could tell us anything, so I refused to believe them. This was uncharted territory, though. We didn't know what to do or say, or how to act. We didn't know what was best for Sean. After the relapse, when I was ready to talk about death, he had already built a wall of silence. Sean wanted to protect us from what he may have already known in his heart: that he was going to die.

We went to Parents' Weekend at the Air Force Academy in Colorado Springs over Labor Day. It was all right, but I cried during most of the flight, both to and from, and Tyler was not much fun to be around. I know he is unhappy and has gone through some difficult times. The day after we discovered Sean's cancer had metastasized while he was still in treatment, Tyler had to leave for six weeks of basic training at the Academy. Tyler and I had driven to Al's office the previous night, and we told him before breaking the news to Sean.

The following morning, Tyler was shipped off to his own kind of hell, and he was miserable. We were not able to accompany him, because after he boarded the plane, I immediately had to take Sean to Salt Lake City. Tyler was on his own. He wrote some sweet letters during basic training, though, about how much he loved us and how he had not realized we were such a close family until he left home. I was amazed at his observation. I thought we were like the Brady Bunch, with a cynical edge perhaps, but always loving and close. Maybe Tyler didn't see it that way.

He encouraged his little brother to tell him everything and was specific about his request, but Sean was only able to write a couple of times before he became too ill to lift a pencil. We finally telephoned Tyler when it was obvious Sean was dying and it was going far too fast.

We were afraid that if we brought Tyler home during basic training to watch Sean die, he would quit the Academy. We didn't let on how bad things were. But suddenly this course of action seemed wrong, and Dr. Adrian and his compassionate nurse, Letti, made a house call in order to convince us that we needed to let Tyler know.

We were surprised at the empathy the Air Force Academy offered. I don't know what I was expecting, a strict and unfeeling military attitude perhaps, but I was mistaken. They offered to take Tyler to the airport the night we called, insisting he come home and take all the time he needed for the services. They were understanding and provided a safe emotional avenue for Tyler to express his initial shock and grief. I think he needed that before returning home, two days prior to Sean's death.

We didn't have the right to make such a monumental decision for our eldest son. When I picked him up at the airport, he asked bewilderedly, "Were you ever going to tell me?"

"We weren't sure you would want to be home right now," I argued in a small voice.

"That's stupid," Tyler answered. "Of course I want to be here." We had underestimated him. We were trying to protect him from the pain, and that is impossible. Hiding from death makes it even more tragic.

As soon as Tyler arrived home, he raced upstairs to see Sean and began singing military songs to him, funny, entertaining ones. Tyler is typically very reserved and in control of his feelings and emotions, so he hasn't done anything like that for years. I think it was his gift to Sean, the only thing he could do for his dying brother, something Sean knew was just for him. Sean was so tired, he could scarcely keep his eyes open, but he smiled happily whenever Tyler was in the room. We unplugged the telephones and spent the evening together, ordering a pizza that Sean couldn't eat and watching a video he was unable to see because of the tumors pressing on his optic nerves. But those were his requests. When he learned Tyler was coming home, he suggested, "Maybe we can have a pizza

SEAN

and video night. That would be like old times."

Sean managed to limp into the bedroom to play a computer game (poker, one of their favorites) with Tyler. It was a supreme effort, but Sean was determined. Al, Hayley, and I laid on the bunk beds and watched, sharply aware that we were witnessing a precious and final moment in our life as a family of five. The following night, Sean slipped into a coma, and on Thursday he died. He was waiting for his brother to get home before he finally let go.

When Tyler arrived at the Academy in June, he attended services at the Protestant Chapel one Sunday, which pleasantly surprised me because we had not raised our children with any particular religion. The famous cathedral with the high pitched ceiling symbolically reaching towards heaven was magical, Tyler said, and he sat down and cried. The outside world seemed harsh and unforgiving, and everything in there was beautiful. Maybe he was touched by God, or perhaps his spiritual side was crying for attention. But now he is suffering, in his own uncommunicative way. He wants to blame us for his decision to attend a military academy, I think, but he hasn't found the words. Tyler loves and respects us and knows we can't handle anything else right now. He, too, is trying to protect us.

Anyway, on Parents' Weekend we went to the Air Force/BYU football game, and I am certain Sean was there. I felt a burning sensation in my heart, like the night he died. The feeling was overwhelming. I could not see him, I could not touch him, so how could he be with me?

September 16, 1995

One of Sean's doctors said he wished we could bottle our son's determination. I have never seen anyone so determined to be happy. Sean watched his life be taken away from him, and he didn't buckle. He invented a new life. No whining, no complaining, he just did it.

I still wonder if I tried hard enough to save Sean's life. A week before he died, we took him to the emergency room with a nosebleed. Chemotherapy had already failed, and there was nothing left to try. We were waiting for the end, and we desperately wanted to avoid the hospital, because they are especially skilled at wasting time and Sean didn't have much left. But we could not stop the bleeding after two hours of pinching his nose until our fingers were numb, and we ended up in the emergency room at 6 a.m.

The emergency physician discovered that Sean's hematocrit and platelets were dangerously low. I didn't want to know that, nor did I want to know that the low counts were not the result of chemo, which had taken place too long ago to have an effect on his blood. We followed our usual routine and ordered platelets to stop the nosebleed and a unit of blood to combat his fatigue.

Al left for work before the pediatrician on call (our doctor was on vacation in Alaska) met me in the corridor outside of Sean's room and accused me of not accepting my son's death.

"Why are you giving him blood?" he asked incredulously.

"It will make him feel better," I answered, exhausted.

"Yes, it will," the doctor agreed with an edge of sarcasm in his voice. "It will also extend his suffering. You really need to speak with a clergyman; you obviously have not accepted what is going to happen to your son."

SEAN

I was insulted and immediately put on the defensive, but it's difficult to be angry at someone who is ignorant of the situation. He hadn't a clue about us and he did not know that I was fully aware Sean was going to die. This doctor was unworthy of an explanation, though he did have a point about the blood, however callously delivered. I didn't want to extend Sean's suffering, so I was faced with another decision: to transfuse or not to transfuse. I wanted Sean to have the platelets, because I didn't want him to bleed to death, but the unit of blood was a sensitive issue. I had to decide, and I was all alone. Al was gone and not available by telephone, and the pediatrician at the hospital was unfamiliar with our family, so I couldn't trust him.

I suddenly realized that Al and I were not seeing Sean as others saw him. His feet had swelled to double their normal size, his body was wasted, his face was white and drawn, the tumors on the back of his head had converged into one huge mass, and there was a new, tennis ball sized tumor at the base of his throat. Add those alarming details to the never ending stream of blood dripping out of Sean's nose, and he looked like he was already dead. But I was still in agony, tormented over whether it was time for Sean's life to end. Why did I have to decide? Why did I have to play God? If I chose not to transfuse him with red blood cells, everything would go quickly and he would die in a few days.

Casey, along with Holly and Kelly (Sean's devoted teacher friends), came to the hospital after they heard Sean was there. Sean was aware of the tension and fear surrounding him, and I think he was worried he might die in that hospital room. If the platelets hadn't stopped the nosebleed, he would have. He would have bled out, as many cancer patients do.

Holly agreed with my final decision not to give Sean

blood and prolong his suffering. "Sean deserves some dignity, Julie," she said. "He has always been so dignified."

A story was shared at his funeral about Sean's first meeting with Holly and Kelly. Sean was at a school activity with Casey, who already knew the teachers well, and they had asked for a ride somewhere. When they got into the car, Casey accidentally shut Sean's hand in the door. "Casey, my hand is in the door," Sean announced quietly. There was no hysteria or screaming, just a simple request. "Open the door, please." We laugh about that now, because it was characteristic of Sean. He didn't fuss about things. He always maintained his dignity. Holly was right.

An old friend who has a boy the age of Sean was working on the pediatric floor that day, and she offered support as well. "Julie, if my son was in that hospital bed looking like Sean does, I would make the same decision you have." Kelly was so sad, she couldn't say anything, and Casey was quietly supportive.

Most of the time I think we did the right thing, but I still vacillate. When I went into Sean's room and told him there would be no blood transfusion (without asking his opinion), he turned to me with wide eyes and asked, "If they don't give me blood, will that kill me?"

Sean was hardly naive. He knew about his disease. He also knew that a falling hematocrit causes severe anemia and eventual congestive heart failure, and when his trusting eyes met my defeated ones, he understood that I had finally given up.

"No, it won't kill you," I answered with inordinate calm. "But your bone marrow is not making those cells anymore." I continued with the clinical explanation, struggling to sound reasonable. But the truth is, I lied to him. Sean asked me a question, and I lied. I cannot live with that, that *I* made a decision to cut his life short. What if a miracle was waiting to happen?   Later on that day, after Al had returned to the hospital, Sean studied his dad and me and said shakily, "You know how much I love you both, don't you?"

Al urged me to transfer the blame to him, because he claimed to agree with my decision. He argued that if Sean was able to be logical, he would have said, "Don't give me the transfusion, just let me go." But I am not sure of that, and I never will be. I often wonder if Al would have made the same decision if I had not made it for him.

In answer, perhaps, to my continued guilt, I had a dream last night about Sean dying from the cancer, not from congestive heart failure like he finally did, which happens if there is not enough blood circulating through the body. In my dream, I watched Sean suffer and die an inch at a time, red-faced, swollen, and fully aware of his discomfort. I wonder if I was seeing the worst case scenario, what might have happened if we had given him blood that day and decided to allow him a slower death from the cancer alone.

Today I was in the book store, uselessly debating with myself over whether I had done the right thing for Sean, and I was looking at books about death in the New Age section. I selected one at random, a paperback about near death experiences by Dr. Melvin Morse. It was rather lengthy, and I just happened to open it to a page near the end of the book. What I read, a mother's account of watching her son die at home from cancer, answered my endless guilt. Following is part of the account, the words that seemed to jump off the page and into my heart.

> I really believe that if the parents are not
> ready or willing to let the child go, then the

dying can drag on and on... Most parents that I've talked to were not like us, though. They wanted to try everything up to the bitter end, even if there was almost no chance. These parents seem to have a harder time grieving.

One lady that I have been writing to has an eight year old daughter who died of leukemia. The doctors told her it was fatal, but she said they wanted to try it all. That girl went through hell. She was in the hospital for most of her last six months while doctors tried radiation, chemotherapy, and all kinds of things. Just before the girl died, she said: "I failed. I'm sorry."

After Sean died no one wanted to talk about it. Most Americans are terrified about death. It leaves us bereaved parents in a very bad state.

Transformed By The Light
—Melvin Morse, M.D. 1992
Ivy Books

There is certainly no right or wrong during times like these (when the doctors told me that I wanted to punch them in the face), but reading this mother's words helped me come to terms with what we had decided to do, or at least begin to. There is an interesting footnote: her son's name was *Sean* too. I wonder if this was more than coincidence.

SEAN

September 20, 1995

I found the short story that Holly said Sean had written for an assignment in her class several months before he died. It was in a pile of his school papers, and concerns a mother whose teenaged son dies of cancer. As the story progresses, she is diagnosed with the same disease. She's ready to surrender to death, when her dead son appears at the foot of her hospital bed and says it is not her time to die, and she must not give up. She survives, and in the final scene of the story, is fully recovered and sitting on a park bench enjoying the sunshine. Her angel son appears and sits down beside her. He asks his mother for a promise. She swears she would do anything for him, and soberly he issues his request. "Be happy, Mom."

I suppose that was meant for me: a pretty tall order, Sean. Happiness doesn't seem to be my right, but I will try. Just be patient.

September 26, 1995

Sean sometimes had uncontrollable nosebleeds, when the chemo had destroyed his platelets and there was nothing to stop the bleeding. One late night, Al and I took him to the emergency room, where the doctor and nurse struggled to stem the flow of blood. The doctor had just removed a huge clot from Sean's nose, when we heard a loud thump. Al had fainted from the sight of the blood clot and dropped to the floor. The doctor and nurse abandoned their patient, who still had blood dripping from his nose, and rushed to Al's side.

Sean shook his head indulgently. "Dad's such a lightweight," he said with a smile.

September 27, 1995

Casey's mom shared a story about something that happened last year when Casey and Sean went to a movie together. A group of kids were teasing Sean about his bald head (they didn't know him) and Casey jumped on their case, threatening to fight them for his friend. Sean, in his typically silent fashion, had not shared it with us. It reminds me of something that happened in Kelly's class, when Sean returned to school after the relapse. She had a new student who didn't know Sean and was not aware he had cancer. When the boy spotted Sean's hairless head, he yelled, "Hey, are you a skinhead, part of the militia or something?"

Since the militia is a white supremacist group and Sean has a close friend who is black, that was especially embarrassing. Kelly started laughing, which was good, because it helped Sean regard the boy as ignorant rather than cruel. Our son got a taste of what it was like to be different during the two years of his illness.

September 28, 1995

Hayley's eighth birthday is today. We had a private

celebration at home with just Al and me. Last year, Sean helped me give a party for his little sister. We planned the agenda and refreshments, and it was lots of fun. Twelve hyperactive girls were in our house, jumping off the sofa and giggling. Sean was here too, helping with prizes and games, but today he was not, and neither was Tyler. Our family is gone. Where did they go? How could we be torn apart so suddenly?

My sister Mary called to wish her niece a happy birthday, and I could not stop crying. I held myself together all day, for Hayley's sake, though I strongly felt something wasn't right. I kept trying to ignore it, hoping the feeling of doom would go away, but when Mary telephoned, I couldn't contain it any longer. A simple birthday, not even Sean's, for God's sake, is a reminder of what we have lost.

OCTOBER

SEAN

They that love beyond the world
cannot be separated by it.
Death cannot kill what never dies.

—William Penn

October 2, 1995

I feel removed, invisible, like I am living in another dimension. Things are going on around me, but they don't seem real. Everything seems unimportant. What is all this chaos about? Did God simply decide to throw us down here for fun? Surely he knew that some of us wouldn't make it, that life would prove to be too much. Was his plan experimental, or was there a method to such madness?

Nothing seems worth bothering with now. I spend all my time reading, because anyone's world seems better than this one, and when I can force myself, I write. I do not know what will become of me.

We are deep into the heavy pain. We were so prepared for the *idea* of Sean's death that it wasn't a shock when he died. The shock set in two years ago when Al and I were standing in a hospital room at Primary Children's in Salt Lake City, Utah, and the doctors told us Sean's cancer was widespread. The night we arrived at the emergency room three and a half hours away from home, I knew it was bad, but we had no definite diagnosis. Al hoped that the following day would bring better news. We left Sean in the intensive care unit at 1 a.m. and rented a nearby hotel room, falling exhausted into bed. Al held me while I cried. "Let's just wait and see," he said soothingly. He finally went to sleep, but I couldn't. I returned to the hospital at 4:00 a.m. to check on Sean, worried that the high calcium in his blood (elevated because the cancer had spread to his bones) might create serious heart problems. But he was stable and sleeping heavily.

The following day, it was my turn to comfort Al. When Dr. Adams told us the scans confirmed Sean had cancer and that it was extensive, Al began to cry, heavy, deep sobs of betrayal and pain. I hugged him tight, and we held each other, struggling to collect ourselves before we told Sean.

We were past shock. There was no buffer zone when Sean died, only the deep abyss of a new reality staring us coldly in the face.

October 4, 1995

I have lost the fight in me. I had it when Sean was alive, the ability to feel passionate about things and try to make them right. One night during his illness, we went out to dinner with Mark and Ann, our friends from Boise. The meal was dreadful, ranging from overcooked to inedible. "Let Julie take care of it," Al suggested. "She's really good at this sort of thing."

Whenever I got upset about something at home, Al jokingly warned the kids, "Mom's getting out the heavy artillery. Stay clear."

I obliged my dinner companions and complained about the food, and the owner of the restaurant charged us half, or maybe he didn't charge us at all. I cannot remember the details, but we all laughed at Ann's observation. "Don't mess with a mom who has a child with cancer."

That was how I used to be. I went to bat for my family, and I often won. Problems were challenges, circumstances I could fix. But now I understand that the big things are out of my control. I can't fix everything, and I no longer want to. I am unable to muster up the energy or desire for a conflict. It is simply not worth it.

Life is not fair. We don't always get what we want. Period. I want to reach a point in my existence in which my personal concerns, what I did and didn't get in this life, don't matter anymore.

That would be an overwhelming relief.

October 5, 1995

Nights are difficult for me, but they were during Sean's illness too. Whenever he was hospitalized and I didn't stay through the night, I always telephoned around 1 or 2 a.m. to ask if he was all right. I hoped my calls would encourage the nurses to check on him more often. When I was not with Sean I worried that something bad would happen, that he would wake up feeling really sick and forget to push the call light for the nurse, or that, worse, he would die alone - - without me. There was no end to the things that could happen, and nighttime compounded the possibilities.

Whenever I left Sean home alone, if I had to pick Hayley up from school or go to the store, I was terrified that he would have a crisis while I was gone. When I heard sirens, I was sure they were heading to our house, and I always half expected to pull into our driveway and see an ambulance. It never happened, but the fear was constant. Now I am having trouble sleeping at night, like Sean did. When he was in the hospital, he had to have intravenous Ativan or he could not fall asleep. During the final weeks of his life, he used medication every night to help him relax before bedtime.

Did Sean have trouble sleeping because he was afraid he wouldn't wake up? Another theory to torture myself with.

October 6, 1995

I am alone with my grief. I wonder where God is, because he seems to have deserted me. I wonder if it matters whether I'm sad rather than happy. Perhaps the Buddhist belief in the eternal cycle of suffering is closer to the truth. I can only exist, try to function, and act cheerful when Tyler telephones. That is the most I can hope for.

Two years ago, Sean's cancer was diagnosed after visiting local doctors for over three weeks and coming up with nothing. When the original malignant tumor was removed and examined, the doctors said it could be one of three kinds of cancer. Two strains were less aggressive and easier to treat, but Sean's cancer was finally identified as the worst of the three, the one with the poorest prognosis. It was Rhabdomyosarcoma, Stage IV, a rare muscle cancer that originated in his right testicle.

The nightmare began with complaints of right thigh pain when I picked him up from football practice a week after school started. He limped to the car, crying. Sean was not a baby; he was a tough, athletic twelve year old and had just finished playing the summer season of little league baseball and travelling with the all-star team. Sean was much healthier than our other children, I thought. He seldom got sick and went on high from morning 'til night, never letting up.

I thought he had pulled a muscle, so the following day we began the round of doctor visits. I had scheduled professional photographs of the kids that day as well, something I had never been able to afford before. I kept joking that Sean was going to have his leg in a cast or something so we'd better get them done right away. I definitely felt an urgency. Now we have these beautiful photographs of Sean, and of the three children together. I am so grateful I didn't cancel. The day after that, things began falling apart quickly.

The first doctor visit indicated that Sean's limp was nothing to worry about. An orthopedic physician took x-rays, ordered lab work, and thought it was a viral infection. He told us to go home and let Sean rest for a few days. Sean stayed down, but the pain worsened and moved into his back. It became so severe that he couldn't walk and was finally reduced to crawling into the bathroom on his hands and knees. I took him to a different orthopedic doctor, who seemed more determined to get to the bottom of it. I was grateful someone was taking Sean's complaints seriously, but by that time the cancer was widespread, permeating his bones and bone marrow. That was causing the bone pain, though we didn't know it then.

The orthopedist ordered a bone scan, which came out normal, but later on we learned it was read incorrectly by the hospital radiologist. The lab work was normal too, but a spot showed up on the kidneys and the orthopedist referred us to a local urologist. Sean had an IVP, a test to determine how well the kidneys are functioning, at the hospital. He had to drink mag citrate beforehand, and it made him vomit. We visited the urologist after the results came back, and he said the kidneys were healthy. "Sean has *growing pains*," he announced cheerfully. "Nothing more."

When a child is unable to bend over and touch his toes and can barely walk, I would not attribute it to growth. But the truth is that his kidneys were not the problem— not at that time, anyway.

Sean continued throwing up the rest of the day, and the following day was worse. It became a continuous bout with nausea and vomiting, 25 to 30 times on that Tuesday. Clearly, this was no longer the mag citrate. My mother was visiting then, and she urged us to see our regular pediatrician. There was a strange virus circulating in our area, and the symptoms included periods of vomiting and dehydration, accompanied by back pain. We consoled ourselves briefly with the idea that this was only a virus. Dr. Adrian, our pediatrician, whose son was a classmate and friend of Sean's, was thorough in his examination, but he had nothing new to offer. The symptoms were puzzling, and lab work continued to be normal.

After a few days, we returned to our pediatrician's office. Sean was losing weight rapidly, and though he would have days when he felt better, the troublesome symptoms always returned. If his doctor couldn't come up with a diagnosis by the end of the week, we planned to take Sean to Primary Children's in Salt Lake City, Utah. Dr. Adrian agreed and had Sean hospitalized. We spent three days in our local hospital, where they ran numerous tests, revealing nothing definitive. Dr. Adrian was persistent in conferring with other physicians, and he found a hydrocele (a water filled sac) around Sean's testicle. Naturally, he believed the hydrocele was related to the symptoms, and a surgeon was consulted.

The surgeon examined Sean two or three times, but he couldn't see anything inside the hydrocele other than a normal sized testicle inside the sac. An ultrasound wasn't ordered, as it should have been, and the surgeon predicted Sean would get better on his own. I might have excused his incompetence, because I know this was something they hadn't seen before and it *was* puzzling, but I could not excuse the way he treated Sean. The surgeon grilled our sick boy about when the hydrocele appeared, which Sean refused to share. He was a shy and modest 12 year old, and very ill. When he didn't cooperate, the doctor became rude. Sean loved and appreciated most of his physicians, but he disliked that man from the start.

Even now, it's hard for me to control my bitterness when I see him speeding around in his sports car with the convertible top down, seemingly without a care in the world. I didn't confront him about how he treated our son, though. All my energy was focused on Sean, and I figured that what was done was done. It was never our intent to make people pay for their errors in misdiagnosing Sean. Perhaps most of them did the best they could. Medicine certainly isn't an exact science. I only wish that more doctors would simply admit that they don't know the answer, and then try to find someone who does.

Sean was hydrated with IV fluids and discharged from the hospital, but on the drive home we had to stop the car so he could vomit by the side of the road. Whatever he had, I knew it was still there.

I remember telling my mother that I could not imagine how families with chronically ill children who had frequent hospitalizations managed to survive. I also recall meeting a family in the oncology clinic a few weeks after Sean's initial diagnosis. Their son had leukemia and they asked how long our child had been in treatment. "Four weeks," I answered tiredly. "What about your son?"

"Four years," they said, faintly hopeful. "But we're waiting for a bone marrow transplant, and maybe that will be the answer to our prayers."

My heart sunk. I was exhausted after only a month, and this family had been going through treatment for *four* years. How would I feel then? I wondered. The hospital was sucking the life out of me - - not to mention Sean. But the time in the hospital was nothing compared to what I am going through now. At least Sean was alive, and there was some hope for the future.

I have an occasional good day and think that maybe, just maybe, I am coming out of this deep, dark well of depression, but the next day is twice as bad. I am standing in quicksand, and I can't find my way out. I may have to spend a long time just going through the motions, trying to be nice to people but sometimes finding it is not worth the effort. "I'm sad and I miss Sean," is all I have to say. At present, that sums up my life. A smile won't come, but tears will, *rivers* of tears. I can summon them up at any time.

Seeing one of Sean's old friends will trigger the pain, or finding a Christmas gift he would have wanted. I saw the new Calvin and Hobbes treasury at a store today, and I started to cry. I spotted the sequel to the book *Jurassic Park* and a new 3-D puzzle, and I could barely contain my grief. People were staring at me, wondering why that crazy lady was crying over comic strip characters like Calvin and Hobbes, as I muttered under my breath, *"I'm sorry, Sean. I am so sorry this had to happen. I'm sorry you can't have Christmas with us anymore. I am sorry for everything!"* On some disturbed level, I still think it is all my fault. I know that's irrational, but I do not understand where he went and why he can't come home. I am desperate to have him back.

All right, so I didn't lose everything. I know there

are many people who have endured more than I have, and that should ease the pain. But it doesn't. Both of my grandmothers lost two children. Knowing that, I should, perhaps, feel better about my own situation, but I don't. My maternal grandmother lost her firstborn child due to a difficult delivery (more specifically, the doctor who came to the house was drunk when he delivered the little girl) and she lost another daughter at two, from pneumonia. My paternal grandmother, Maude, my namesake, lost a son later in life to alcoholism, and a little girl at two, to an infected burn. How did they cope? Not well, I would imagine, and I feel their empathy almost daily.

I feel for others, too, especially those who are in real trouble. A woman telephoned the other day to express her sympathy over our loss. She had read Sean's obituary and knows the family of one of his friends. I have never met this person, but she lost a severely handicapped child six months ago and is aware of my pain.

"While other little girls were going to ballet lessons or soccer games," she explained sadly, "my daughter couldn't even walk or talk." She desperately wants to have some kind of mystical contact, but doubts it will ever happen. "I just want a concrete experience," she said longingly.

Me too. I would love to see Sean again, but I am afraid he's really gone, expect for the feeling in my heart. Is that all I get?

At the end of the conversation, the woman shared that her son had been in cancer treatment but was in remission. Suddenly, I felt lucky and overcome with deep empathy for this stranger. She had lost one child and nearly lost another. What agony! I cannot imagine surviving any more grief than I feel now. People do, I suppose, but you don't have to be happy to survive. You just have to avoid killing yourself. At least I'm winning on that one.

I am aware of my blessings and trying to be grateful for them. I still have Hayley, Tyler, and Al, and I love them all deeply. My gratitude for what I have left should be a consoling factor, but I want Sean, and I cannot help thinking that I didn't try hard enough to keep him alive, that there was something else I could have done to help him. I cut his life short because I wanted his suffering to be over.

I wanted his suffering to be over so that mine could start.

October 7, 1995

I wish I could be the old me again, when I was working full time, raising three active children, managing an enduring marriage and Al's demanding work schedule, and cheerfully thinking that I had never been happier. But that person is gone and I can't bring her back. Life is never going to be all right again. Sean is not coming back, and the longer I remain here on earth, the more people I'm going to lose. Maybe I will lose Al, Tyler, and Hayley. Maybe I'll be the last one left alive in my family, and that will be my punishment. But what am I being punished for? How am I going to get through the rest of this life without letting Sean's death devastate me? Go ahead, God, give me the answer to that.

October 8, 1995

I hate it when people say, "Life goes on," because it doesn't. When you lose someone you love, life does not go on. It stops. I don't want to hear people talk about how they received a miracle either. Someone who knew about Sean told me his sister had Stage IV cancer and has been in remission for years. He believes miracles do happen, yes indeed. Does that mean Sean wasn't good enough for a miracle? Why couldn't we get one too? I know people are not aware of what they are saying, but those things hurt. Another woman whose granddaughter is in remission from cancer said, "Oh, she would never give up. She is just too tough to let this get her."

So what does that make Sean? He was tough and determined as well. Don't tell me your child has a will to live that Sean didn't have. He desperately wanted to live, and he didn't get to.

October 9, 1995

I am acutely aware of other people's tragedies. I remember seeing a poster of a missing child when Sean was initially diagnosed. I shuddered in horror and mumbled, "At least it's not that." But what do those parents say? Having a missing or murdered child is the worst fate of all. I am grateful that Sean was able to die with his family around him. We were lucky to be granted that one small grace.

SEAN

Al was at the cabin again last weekend. I resent that cabin, because building it took Al away from Sean during those final weeks. It is not finished yet and won't be for a while, but Al works on it every weekend. Pounding nails and occupying his mind every moment of each day has helped him deal with the overwhelming grief. But when he is gone, I feel all alone.

Sean was excited about having a cabin nestled in the Sawtooth Mountains. We bought what may be one of the last pieces of affordable land in the Idaho wilderness over two years ago, with the intention of building a small vacation home the following year. Al planned to do all the work, with help from a few relatives. It was a primal desire for my hardworking husband, and the need to claim a piece of the wilderness wouldn't go away, so I finally conceded defeat. Plans to build a cabin proceeded, though I couldn't conceive of being able to afford a second home when it was so difficult to pay for the first. But Sean got sick and had the bone marrow transplant, so everything was delayed.

In May of this year, we decided to build during the summer, afraid that if we waited until next year, Sean wouldn't be alive to see the cabin that had become a part of his dreams too. After the logs were stacked, Sean's cancer metastasized for the last time. The project had exceptionally bad timing, but Al was heavy into the construction and the roof had to be completed before he could stop. His brother-in-law and some of his family helped with the initial phase, but they finally had other commitments. My friend Tris came to the rescue, offering the services of her husband, as well as those of her school principal (who used to be mine as well), to enclose the cabin. Al was able to close things up, a couple of weeks before Sean died.

After the roof was finished, Sean asked tentatively,

"Is Dad going up to the cabin next weekend?"

"No," I answered, "everything's on hold. Your dad just wanted to finish it so we could spend some time there together - - as a family."

"It's too late for that," Sean said soberly.

He was right. It was too late. I harbored some irrational resentment towards Al throughout Sean's illness, and I couldn't get rid of it. I resented him for building a cabin during those critical weeks. Who cared about having a vacation home? Why did my husband insist on acting like nothing had happened? But in all fairness, I had agreed with his decision to build the cabin. I had given my stamp of approval, hoping Sean had more time, so it was my fault too, wasn't it? Where was all this anger coming from?

I also resented being left to deal with the endless details of Sean's treatment because Al had to work. But what was the alternative? *Someone* had to support the family, and it wasn't easy for Al to leave Sean and help other people in his psychotherapy practice. I'm sure there were times when he couldn't face another problem, but he had to. He always bore up.

To illustrate the constant demands in Al's life, the morning after Sean died, he had an adoption study scheduled at 7 a.m. He couldn't cancel because the people were leaving town that day, so he had to go, in spite of the horrors of the previous night and the heavy weight on his heart. These people were angry because they had telephoned Al's office the day before and he hadn't returned their call. Al responded in his characteristically quiet way, "I'm sorry. But my son died last night."

He hasn't gotten a break from all the stress, and after Sean died, my bitterness melted away. It was like a miracle. I wasn't angry anymore. I no longer blamed Al for deserting me, an unfair and illogical recrimination, and I knew he didn't deserve harsh judgment from me. He lost a son too, and he adored Sean.

The other night, Al and I were talking about Sean's death and whether it would continue to cast a shadow on the rest of our lives. "Given a choice," I offered bitterly, "I wouldn't repeat this life. It is too hard and too sad. I am disappointed that things have turned out this way. Whatever I have left now, it's just not good enough to make up for everything I've lost."

I was fairly sure Al would agree with me, but he said, "Oh, I don't know. I've had a good life. Outside of Sean's death, it's been pretty good. I think I would do it again. All in all, I have been happy."

I stared at him in amazement. Al had found a bright side to all this darkness. How could he do that? I wondered bewilderedly.

Now I understand where Sean's optimism came from. Sean, who loved his life in spite of how it had turned out, had a similar outlook to his dad's. They shared the belief that this life is worth the effort. Their glass is always half full, not half empty. I didn't realize they were so alike, until now.

October 14, 1995

Tyler telephoned last night, and we had a much needed talk. I know that our eighteen, soon to be nineteen, year old son misses Sean, who was five years younger, and that he's desperately sad about what happened, but he hasn't talked about it. Last night was different. He opened up - - just a little. He feels guilty and sad, almost everything I feel. I've often wondered if Tyler was capable of feeling deep emotions, and my perception of him cast a chill on our relationship. I worried that he was little affected by what happened to his younger brother, because sometimes he acted like he didn't care. It hardened my attitude towards him, and I didn't like feeling that way, especially since I was wrong. Tyler does feel the sadness and pain of our loss, but he doesn't express it like I do. I'm operating under the illusion that I have the corner on all the grief in this family.

Last night Tyler cried over the telephone, and I think he wanted me to share that I thought Sean's death was unfair and dreadfully sad and that it was terrifying to see him die, because that's how he feels. He may believe, deep down, that Sean is with God, but my surviving son is still devastated by the experience, as we all are. I've been busy comforting Tyler, Hayley, and Al, trying to convince them (and myself) that this was one of those things that was meant to happen, but I have overlooked their agonizing pain. I've focused on the blessing of having Sean die at home with his family around him, and tried too hard to point out the positive aspects of his death: that he had a profound influence on others and his life was worthwhile. But it doesn't change the fact that his death was heart wrenching, and it doesn't fix anything.

Tyler and Al remember seeing our little boy struggle for every breath that final day, swollen and suffering, white and nearly lifeless. Hayley remembers singing songs to her dying brother and holding his unresponsive hand. She was fearless. Sean didn't look anything like himself, but the seven-year-old child did not back away. They are still wrapped up in the cruelty of it all. I can't deny them their feelings, because I feel that way too. I think Tyler was relieved when I said, "Yes, it was horrible and terrifying, and we're not going to know why Sean had to die - - not in this lifetime."

There's no reason good enough to warrant such suffering.

October 16, 1995

I know this is hard to believe, but Sean was here last night. I obviously won't be telling many people about this, because no one would believe me. I can hardly believe it myself. I was lying in bed around 11:00 p.m., sleepless as usual, and Al was snoring beside me. I suddenly felt a burning sensation in my chest. I wondered if it was heartburn, which I've never had before, but quickly decided that couldn't be it, because the feeling was exceptionally warm and it didn't hurt. I got out of bed and stepped into the living room, where I sat on the sofa and felt the burning sensation grow stronger. I knew without a doubt that Sean was with me.

His presence was overpowering, like it was after the mortuary attendants took his body away the night he died. I couldn't see him, but that didn't seem to matter, because a sweet, healing power spread through my body. I felt incredibly relaxed and no longer worried about what had happened to him. I talked to Sean, and he communicated things as well, but I didn't hear his voice. It was like telepathy, and the words he communicated, actual sentences, were in my head. Sean was strangely evasive about what my future held. At one point, when I said I was considering adopting a child and wondered if it was the right thing to do, he hesitated before communicating to me that I would figure it out on my own. Thanks, Sean.

I suppose I want another child so I can have my family back. But it won't be the *same* family I had before, and that's what I want.

The mother of a friend of Hayley's, who lost a child to cancer a few years ago, went through similar struggles concerning adoption, finally deciding against it. She was emotionally fragile after the death of her small daughter, and if something went wrong with the adoption, she didn't know if she would be able to cope. I've decided to give my grief a year before I make any major life commitments. I need some floating time.

Last night I had the overwhelming impression that Sean is happy and content and approves of my change of heart over the past few days. I've been writing and feeling a little better. I know he does not want to be the source of my pain. He doesn't want to keep me in this hole of despair. I know that life is all about picking yourself up and moving on, but I can't hold on to that belief yet.

Sean was trying to encourage me and tell me that changes are coming, but patience is required, as usual. I don't know why he chose that particular time to come, except that my spirit feels a wee bit healthier now, like I might survive. Perhaps he wanted to remind me that he'll continue to look after me, and that I have to listen deep in my heart to feel his presence. It's not something I'm going to find on the surface, because Sean is beyond this life. He's immortal, good, and full of love. I wonder if we realized what a beautiful child we had until he got sick.

I sat with Sean's spirit for over an hour, but in spite of the magical feeling, I became sleepy. Suddenly, I spotted something out of the corner of my eye passing into our bedroom, a flash of ivory colored material. I have been thinking about this, trying to decide whether it was my imagination, but have finally decided to accept it. Holly said, "If you have to talk yourself out of believing it happened, it must have."

    I returned to the bedroom, as if I were following Sean, and eased myself into bed. We listened to his dad's snoring routine, and Sean's silent laughter surrounded me. Listening to their dad snore has always been a source of amusement for our kids. Sean embraced me with his warmth and soothed me into a peaceful sleep.

    When I woke up this morning, I continued to feel his presence, though it wasn't as strong. Maybe he's so good that some of him lingers on.

    "Sean was here last night," I announced as Al was leaving for work. I didn't think he would believe me, but he did, without hesitation.

October 20, 1995

    I might have known several good days in a row would come to an end, a crashing halt, actually. I feel like shit, I look worse (it's pretty bad to look worse than shit), and furthermore, I don't care. I cannot bear for things to continue like this, but if I don't have the energy to change them, who can? I am exhausted, too exhausted to change a thing, too exhausted to do anything but suffer.

    I miss Sean desperately. I love him so much. While he was alive, I wasted my time working on a novel that is never going to be published, and I missed out on Sean's life. Writing for two or three hours a day was too much. I doubt that I impressed him with my work ethics, and besides, who cares about having work ethics? I can't get anything done now.

    Didn't I realize how precious our time was and that

I could *never, ever* bring it back? The last six months of Sean's life, I wrote very little, but I did not enjoy every second I should have. Was I successful in making my statement about trash television by refusing to watch it with him? Well, hooray for me. I am proud I was such a fine example. Now I would give anything to sit down and watch a television program with Sean, and I would love it, because I love everything about him, every corner of his mind and every shadow of his soul. I had no idea how bereft I would feel when he was gone.

I wish we had done professional photos again after Sean lost his hair, because that is how I remember him. I thought I wouldn't want a visual reminder of our sick son, but I regret my lack of foresight. I want to remember it all. I want to see Sean at his most beautiful, without hair, with the pale, angular face and skinny body, and the effervescent smile. Last night Al brought his dinner into the bedroom and set his plate on the desk in front of a framed photo of Sean. He wanted to have dinner with his smiling son.

I am bone tired, with no zip at all. I have even been sleeping in the afternoons, which I have never done before. I simply cannot stay awake. Maybe if I give in to it for a while, I will get caught up. The other night, I fell asleep while I was sitting up. I was drifting off when I heard Hayley say, "Is she asleep?" I opened my eyes, and she and Al were staring at me. There is no reasonable explanation for this fatigue, a year ago maybe, but not now. My life has suddenly become easier, other than the intense grief. The other day I cried all day and night, and wondered if I was going to cry like that for the rest of my life. It was uncontrollable.

Casey, Sean's best friend, stopped by today. I love that boy, and I love what he did for Sean. Sean was able to count on Casey's friendship and it was a comforting anchor. Casey's birthday was yesterday, and when he came over, he had tears in his eyes. "I believe Sean is okay, but I want him back. It's selfish, I know, but I still want him back." My feelings exactly.

Today is Tyler's nineteenth birthday. We sent him money, tucked inside a pathetic birthday card. He can't use anything at the Academy this year - - no music, videos or clothes, so there is no point in buying gifts. I think it will be depressing for him, the first year of adult birthdays. I always get vaguely depressed on my birthday, and I don't know why. I am not sad about getting older, but a child's birthday is a special time. When you become an adult, it is just another day, and maybe that makes me sad. My thoughts are with Tyler today, though I am relieved he isn't here to celebrate. Hayley's birthday depressed the hell out of me.

Something good has happened, though. For the first time in my life since I left the church I was raised in, I have a personal relationship with God. When I gave up religion, I thought I had to relinquish my spirituality. It doesn't have to be that way. I wish I had not allowed myself to be misinformed, because I didn't teach my children to pray and I failed to help them explore their spiritual natures. Introspection is essential in order to survive this life, and praying to a higher being is a part of that. Sometimes God is the only one who listens to you.

I used to roll my eyes heavenward when people talked about God like he was their best friend. Oh sure, I thought cynically, the idea of a creator is fine, but we have to meet life's challenges on our own. Now I see it differently, though I like to keep my beliefs private. Everyone has to form their own theories about God and how he fits into their lives, and it doesn't matter whether his name is

Buddha, Mohammed, or Jesus. It is the same entity, the same higher spiritual being. I am accustomed to calling him God, but his name could be Sam or Ethel, and it would not matter.

We received direct spiritual guidance when Sean was dying. I went for a solitary walk a week before he died, and on the way home, I sat down under a tree and asked whoever happened to be listening up there, "How much longer is this going to continue? Is he going to suffer indefinitely?"

A few hours later, Sean was in the hospital with a nosebleed, and we discovered that his red blood cells and platelets were critically low because his bone marrow was not producing those cells anymore. His marrow was full of cancer. When we made the painful decision not to transfuse him, Dr. O'Brien from Salt Lake predicted Sean had a week left. That was exactly what he had; I had received my answer.

There was more spiritual intervention the night Sean died. He was in a coma and struggling for each breath, and I gathered Al, Hayley, and Tyler along the edge of the sofa where Sean laid. We held hands and asked God to release our anguished boy from his body and end his torment. Minutes later, Sean took his last breath.

It was not coincidence. It was a direct answer.

But sometimes I get angry at God. Why did Sean have to go through what he did, and what was the point? I cannot understand why children have to suffer. Last year, a little girl from New York City was beaten to death by her mother, and the story of her life and death haunts me. The child was full of light and love but was tortured by a hateful, evil guardian on this earth. The only consolation is that the beautiful little girl is getting all the love she needs now. God is wrapping her up in his arms and loving her until she is fully healed. I am certain of that.

In relation to my own heartache, which seems minor in comparison, I have never asked "Why me"? Instead, I have always wondered, "Why *not* me"? What makes me so special, and did I really think I could escape tragedy? No, of course not. But I need help coping with the residual shock, and I feel the empathy of spiritual beings watching over me. I am closer to God than I have ever been, and it was not religion that created this bond.

It was Sean.

October 28, 1995

There is a light at the end of the tunnel, but sometimes it is very dim. Last night I went into Sean's bedroom because I noticed the double closet doors were open. Hayley opens the doors to get drawing paper from the inside shelf and always forgets to close them afterwards. Sean's few belongings are on the shelves, including the red quilt his grandmother made him when he was a little boy. The quilt always smelled like Sean and was rarely washed because he wrapped up in it every day. The night he died, I held his quilt up to my tear-stained face so I could smell it and take him in. It was the last tangible evidence that Sean had been here, that he had been real and was once ours to love. But the following night Tyler slept with it, and I was so disappointed. It no longer smelled like Sean. I couldn't bring the scent back, so I gloomily washed and folded the quilt and set it on the closet shelf where it has not been touched since.

Last night I noticed an odd but familiar smell in the

bedroom closet, and I started sniffing all the clothes inside. I must have looked insane, carefully inhaling the scents within those double doors. But I had washed everything after Tyler returned to school, and each folded and hung item smelled vaguely of detergent. When I held Sean's favorite quilt, the one I had washed, folded, and placed on the shelf after Tyler slept with it, I knew where the smell had originated. I held the blanket up to my face and took him in. Sean was all over that quilt.

I thought about it all day, returning to the closet several times before Al got home from work, reaffirming that I had not imagined it. When Al came into the bedroom to check out the closet, he noticed the distinctive odor at once. He began sniffing the clothes, which he said smelled like detergent, before moving on to the red quilt. He immediately announced that it smelled like Sean, especially the edges, as if our boy had wrapped it around him and happily curled up on his bed or on the sofa.

It must have happened within the last day or so. Hayley opens that closet door every day, and I work on the computer in the same room. I would have noticed the telltale scent. How did this happen, and what does it mean? I have no rational explanation, but I may have found the answer in John Milton's *Paradise Lost*: "Millions of spiritual creatures walk the earth unseen, both when we wake, and when we sleep."

Sean is one of them.

SEAN

NOVEMBER

SEAN

When our second son, Joshua, died,
his death formed a hinge in existence.
Everything that had happened before
led up to it, and everything that has
happened since is only afterwards.

A Welsh Childhood
—Alice Thomas Ellis

November 3, 1995

It is interesting how things work out, like getting the things you want but not when you want them. I got married at 17, after graduating from high school a year early. This was unfashionable, especially where I grew up, in a resort town where people were obsessed with image, experience, and sophistication. Only morons wasted their lives by getting married young, and only if they were pregnant, never by choice. I met Al when I was 15, and three weeks later he proposed, though we didn't get married for another year and a half. The night I met him (he was six years older) I confidently informed my mom that I was going to marry Al Miller. She was silent from shock, I suppose, but somehow I knew it would happen. Over two decades later, it is still the best decision I have made in my life.

A couple of months after the wedding, we moved to Tokyo for a year and taught English to Japanese businessmen and women. I admit that the idea of marrying someone who had no objections to living thousands of miles away, which I was dying to do, was exciting, but that was not the deciding factor. I loved him totally and absolutely. I still want to spend every minute I can with Al, but twenty some years ago everyone thought I was making a serious mistake, except for my older sister. Mary watched Al treat me with love and respect, and she saw how hard he worked to make a living, and somehow she knew I would be okay. I made an unpopular decision and acted against logic and sound advice, but I was the only one who knew what was best for me. Thank God I happened to be right. I know I am the exception to the rule.

Marrying young didn't limit us, as people said it would. Al has encouraged me to take advantage of every opportunity we could afford, though there were many years when we could afford nothing. I spent a month travelling alone in Great Britain when Tyler was three years old, something I had always wanted to do. Al suggested it, in spite of objections from both sets of parents who said that I certainly could not go *alone*. We continued to travel occasionally, though finances were always tight and common sense told us we couldn't afford to step out the front door, but sometimes you have to throw common sense out the window and live with the consequences. I like spontaneity. Too much thinking and planning spoils the excitement of living. Life can be so dreary, but when you have an opportunity for excitement and adventure, you had better seize it while you can.

In between the spontaneity and sporadic adventures, we worked hard. There was no one to help us, and we had only ourselves to rely on. Al received a bachelor's degree in Idaho before we moved to Texas, where he earned a Master's in Social Work. I earned two university degrees, one in Registered Nursing and the second in Elementary Education. While we were attending college in Boise, when Tyler was a baby, we were live-in house parents at a group home for runaway teen-aged girls. It was an extremely difficult situation, but we had to save money for graduate school in Texas, and it was essential that we stick it out for two years. Nine girls lived in the group home, and many of them were only a year or two younger than I was. I continually hid my driver's license so the girls would not discover how old I was. We learned a lot about maintaining a calm, understanding, but firm attitude in the face of hysteria, because these emotional girls had continual problems and depended on us to help them. It was not an easy period in our lives.

After two years at the group home, we left Idaho for Texas, where Al went to graduate school. When he received his master's, we returned to Idaho and Sean was born. I entered the nursing program in Twin Falls and graduated two years later, but I didn't like it very well. I felt driven to finish, though, and worked as a hospital and home health nurse for a couple of years before returning to college to major in education. The time and money spent preparing for a nursing career I had no enthusiasm for seemed like a waste of resources, but when Sean became ill, my reasons for hanging in there became obvious.

The training was invaluable. During the two years of his illness, boxes of medical supplies arrived each month with dressing changes for his broviac and davol central lines, daily heparin and saline flushes to keep them patent, syringes for the G-CSF shots (which boosted his white blood cells), pump, IV tubing, and refrigerated bags of hyperalimentation therapy when he got too thin and needed caloric supplements. It was complicated, but we were lucky I was familiar with some of it. We didn't have to hire a home health or hospice nurse. I was able to do it all.

When I made a decision to switch to education, I quickly learned that I liked teaching children and felt far more comfortable in the classroom than I did in the hospital. I wanted to be home with the kids, though, especially when Hayley was born and we had a busy trio to care for. But our finances wouldn't allow it, and I accepted being a working mom. It was a fine balancing act we managed fairly well, although I knew if anything really bad happened, it would all come crashing down.

SEAN

My coping skills were stretched to the limit.

When Al's private practice in psychotherapy became more successful, I began thinking about taking a year's leave of absence. Hayley (a day care regular) had been sick a lot, and when she was five we discovered she had mononucleosis. I would pick her up from day care, and she would say with a huge yawn, "I can't wait to get home so I can lay down." It was not normal behavior for a five-year-old, and I worried that she had something worse, like leukemia, which her friend's sister had recently died of. I took her to the doctor for an examination, but it was only mono. Months of recovery followed, though, and Hayley's continued delicate health contributed to my eventual decision to take a leave of absence the following year. I hoped I could build her strength back up if she had more time at home.

Al and I went out to lunch one day, in October of my seventh year of teaching, and we were talking about the family visiting Hawaii in the spring. I normally jump at the prospect of travel, but this time, oddly, I didn't. I stared at Al and announced out of the blue, "I don't want to go to Hawaii, I want to take a year off."

I am fortunate to be married to someone who wants me to have whatever I want, if that's possible, and he always trusts my judgment, no matter how many times I have changed college majors or careers. "All right," Al responded calmly. "That sounds good." End of discussion. Al, like Sean, didn't ruminate endlessly over a decision. When it was made, that was all there was to it.

I waited until the following spring to give my notice, but a few weeks later I said, "I don't know whether this is going to be *nice* for our family, or whether my being home will be a necessity, but I know it is the best thing for all of us."

Hayley's physical well being was still a concern. I didn't know it would be our healthy Sean, not Hayley, who ended up with a life threatening illness. It is interesting that Hayley never got sick after Sean was diagnosed. I suppose she knew she couldn't.

A few days after school started at the beginning of my leave of absence, Sean became ill. I firmly believe I was guided, because I didn't think I would ever quit teaching, and perhaps we were blessed when Al's business expanded so he could provide for us without the second income. The point is, I wanted to be at home when the children were younger and I was denied the opportunity. When they were all in school (Hayley was starting kindergarten that year) I had the chance, but it didn't seem like the ideal time. I was wrong about that.

Sometimes I feel bitter, though, that I was not allowed one blissful year of enjoying my husband and children without the stress of managing a two-career household. I was only asking for one year of happiness, and it wasn't permitted. However, I am grateful I was able to stay at home with our sick boy without sending us into bankruptcy.

Sean is gone now and I'm still at home. The timing is wrong, but I appreciate the blessing.

November 10, 1995

It was a rare privilege to be allowed to care for Sean during his two-year battle with cancer, and I don't think I fully understood that when he was alive. I was lucky to be able to take care of him. Instead of viewing his illness as a punishment, as I sometimes did, I now believe that the time with Sean was a reward, because I have learned what real love is. You cannot understand the impact of an eternal gift until it is gone, because at the time, although my love for Sean deepened each day and I was aware of that, there were many days I was exhausted and thought his health problems were a burden. My spiritual vision was impaired by fatigue, and I was unable to see things as they really were. I didn't understand that this had become a mission. Caring for Sean is the most significant thing I have done with my life.

I didn't know I would feel so lost when he was gone, and I did not realize how permanent it would be. It has been far worse than I imagined. Sometimes I cry out in agony because I cannot endure the separation. I sob and I cry and I plead, but there is nothing I can do to change it. He is gone. Life is never going to be good again, and that takes the point out of everything.

I remember watching Sean study himself in the bathroom mirror a couple of months before he died. He had taken off his T-shirt and was wearing a pair of silk boxer shorts, and he was shocked by his haggard appearance. I had become accustomed to his withered looks, at 5'6" and 100 pounds, but Sean rarely saw himself without a shirt covering his bony chest.

"Mom," he said worriedly, "I have to put on some weight. Get some candy bars, nuts, ice cream, and nachos." I don't need much encouragement to buy junk food, so I did. We ate it together, and no matter how much weight I gained, Sean said I looked great. He was forgiving of all my shortcomings. I'm not sure he even noticed them, except for my thighs, of course. They are impossible to miss. One summer day when I was wearing a pair of shorts, Sean jokingly observed, "Mom, your thighs look like the Atlantic Ocean. Lots of waves."

But my sturdy legs, cellulite notwithstanding, are strong and capable. Sean's legs were pencil-thin; he was unable to build his body back up, and he tried so hard. He didn't get rewarded for all the suffering. I hate this life and what it does to the innocent.

The sad thing is, Sean really loved it.

November 14, 1995

I have been sick in bed. I don't know what is wrong, probably nothing, but my right leg hurts and I limp when I walk. I fainted in the bathroom the other night, and I am nauseated too. I almost passed out when I was driving home the other day, and that scared the hell out of me. I pulled off to the side of the road before losing consciousness, opened the door, and hung my head until I felt my equilibrium return. Maybe the grief is affecting me physically. During Sean's illness, my nice complexion turned muddy, and when he got really sick, my cheeks bled, warning me perhaps that I was at the breaking point. I am going to see a doctor today, but I'm not expecting fountains of wisdom. He will undoubtedly say it is nothing.

Later — The doctor thinks I have sciatica, an inflammation of the sciatic nerve in the lower back, which causes either intermittent or continual shooting pain in the hip and leg. Now I can tell my sister I'm *down in the back*, and she will get a chuckle out of that. I have ice packs on my lower back. At least I don't have cancer, which I was beginning to suspect. Nothing is allowed to be minor anymore, because I am always expecting the worst. I need to stay down until the sciatic nerve heals, about four weeks, the doctor said. That should do wonders for my increasing weight. I can lay in bed and eat leftover Halloween candy, read books, and gain a few more pounds. I am glad I have some self esteem not based on my physical appearance, because whenever I look in the mirror I see that I have aged, and not very gracefully.

November 17, 1995

We tend to put Sean on a pedestal, and I have to watch that around Hayley and Tyler. Sean seems perfect now, but he had faults just like the rest of us. When he was younger, he struggled with controlling his temper. He would become hysterical over minor conflicts and say things he didn't mean. Al called him *Ricky* when he acted like that.

"I guess Sean isn't here today," Al would announce offhandedly. "We have *Ricky* instead." Tyler thought Sean's alter ego was hilarious, but I'm not sure Sean did. We laughed about it when he got older, though.

It is impossible not to idealize him now. When we examine the past two years and what he lost as he adjusted to the unwelcome changes in his life, he does seem different from the mainstream. I received a lovely card from a girl who attended his junior high that read, "I didn't know Sean very well, but what I do remember about him is that he always held his head high."

Sean's courageous attitude overrode any minor faults he may have had, and that is what we remember. When

we grieve for someone, maybe we have to idealize them.
I don't think there is anything wrong with that, as long as
I avoid pointing it out endlessly to Tyler and Hayley. But
occasionally Al says, tongue in cheek, when I am singing
Sean's praises, "Who *is* this child you're talking about?"

November 21, 1995

Mary sent me a book, and one of the chapters is
prefaced with, "The prince is dead, and darkness descends
over the land." That is the way my life has been for the
past few months, and I think the darkness will come and
go with different intensities for the rest of my life. There
will always be a feeling that something is not right and
that I don't have the power to fix it. I feel a little better
today, but stepping lightly because I am not sure how long
it will last.

I don't know what I would have done without my
sister over the past two and a half years. Mary understood,
sympathized, and didn't make me feel like a self-indulgent
basket case. I could not always talk to Al, because our
collective grief was so thick that honest communication
was sometimes impossible. When you have a critically
ill child, stress levels skyrocket, and the things you have
always hated about your life are sharply accentuated. Al
and I could be very cold towards each other, and that was
a new state of affairs. We had always been best friends.

I took care of Sean's educational needs, medical and
home–care, drove him to Salt Lake, made frequent
telephone calls to doctors, attended endless appointments,
and took care of the rest of the family. Most of the time,

Al couldn't go with Sean and me because he had to work, and I sometimes resented being left alone with the overwhelming responsibilities. I was lonely as well, but the bills had to be paid.

I am fortunate to have an unselfish sister, who is nearly twelve years my senior, because she became my lifeline. Mary telephoned two or three times weekly, every week of Sean's illness, beginning with a tense call made to the emergency room at Primary Children's when he was diagnosed. They connected her directly to the ER. "What's going on, Julie?" she asked over the line.

"Sean was too sick to stay at home any longer," I answered, surprisingly composed. "He's down to 95 pounds and can't stay on his feet. We had to do something."

"What do they think it is?"

I paused for a moment. "Cancer," I finally offered.

"My hell," Mary said shakily, uncomprehending. That turned out to be a perceptive remark. The diagnosis became a living hell for anyone closely involved with us.

Sean adored his Aunt Mary. We visited her family in California about six weeks before his death, and Mary once again suggested that we spend a day at the train museum in Sacramento. She regularly plans this particular outing when we come to visit, and the kids always refuse to go along. We generally have to trick them into learning something.

But shortly before we left Idaho for our visit, Sean flashed a wide, radiant grin and said, "I think I'll give Aunt Mary a thrill and go to that train museum with her."

Sean had a wry sense of humor, and he tried desperately to have a good time. A few weeks before his death, I was staining our huge deck and he was keeping me company while relaxing in a padded lawn chair. At last, he assessed the situation.

"This is what my life has been reduced to. Watching paint dry."

When we drove to Salt Lake City on that snowy night in November after the cancer came back, a nauseated and uncomfortable Sean told jokes at every stoplight as we made our way slowly up the icy, snow packed streets to the hospital on the hill.

He loved his life, in spite of the shattered childhood dreams. Sean made adjustments, took stock of what was left to take pleasure in, and capitalized on it. Why can't I do the same?

Because I am fully human and Sean was ethereal, as if he had one foot in heaven and the other here on earth.

SEAN

DECEMBER

SEAN

Sadness, stillness in the room
In the middle, a table and a bed.
In the bed, a feverish boy.
His mother sits next to him
with a little book.
She reads him his favorite story
and immediately, the fever subsides.

Illness
—Franta Bass

"I never saw another butterfly..."

Children's Drawings and Poems from
Terezin Concentration Camp, 1942-1944

December 5, 1995

The magic is not there anymore. Perhaps that is what propels you through the first half of your existence: the belief that life is magical and miraculous. Lately, I have been thinking about Sean all the time, and the closer it gets to Christmas, the worse I feel. But I no longer wish he had lived longer with cancer, because his life was becoming lonelier and sadder. I think he was tired of belonging to his mother, though that part of his demanding illness was an up side for me. For a couple of years Sean was really mine. I took care of him, we did everything together, and I rarely had to share him. But he didn't want to be mine anymore. He wanted to have friends and be out with people. He had missed out on the adolescent's rite of passage: becoming independent from one's parents. Regardless of how much Al and I loved Sean and how much he loved us, it was not enough to make up for everything else.

I think God took Sean before his life got any uglier.

December 11, 1995

Books have become my constant companions. Recently, I have read Amy Tan's *Hundred Secret Senses*,

which has prompted me to consider reincarnation, a
lengthy biography of Charlotte Bronte (who watched four
sisters, a brother, and a mother precede her in death, and
when her life took a positive turn with marriage and a
pregnancy, she died as well), Tim Parks' *Italian Neighbors*
and *An Italian Education,* a collection of pioneer children's
diaries, *Smilla's Sense of Snow,* Edna O'Brien's novels
and short stories, and Oscar Hijuelo's *Mr. Ives' Christmas.*
I have also discovered a couple of new authors, like Lisa
St. Aubin de Teran and Alice Thomas Ellis. But when I
want a good laugh, I read Bill Bryson's books. Reading
is the only thing that soothes me.

Last week we saw a touching, spiritual film called
Beyond Rangoon. The main character in the film has
recently lost her husband and child to an act of violence,
and she embarks on a trip to the Orient to distract herself—
but of course, she can't. She befriends an elderly professor,
on the eve of political disaster in Burma. "I thought if I
was good," she said, "and worked hard, that I had a right
to happiness." The Burmese professor answers with
profound words: "We are taught that suffering is the one
promise life always keeps, so that if happiness comes, we
know it is a precious gift, which is ours only for a brief
time."

I am in pain, but perhaps my anguish is just the tip of
a wave among an entire ocean of suffering. I know, at
least for today, that it could have been much worse.

December 13, 1995

Al and I have spent twenty years of marriage planning

for the future. We have raised the kids, struggled with insane work schedules and financial difficulties, and believed it would all turn out fine in the end. Before Sean was diagnosed, we often talked about having several years to enjoy the boys' sports, in which they were actively involved. We were happy it wasn't over with Tyler, and we looked forward to attending Sean's basketball and baseball games throughout junior high and high school. But that did not happen, because Sean was diagnosed with cancer at the beginning of the 7th grade. In one of her books, Anne Lamott wrote, "If you want to make God laugh, tell her your plans."

I have spent my life making plans, but now I prefer to live day by day, with only a vague plan for the future. Anything could happen at any time to screw it all up, and besides, if good fortune comes my way now, it will never be enough. At best, it would be a consolation prize.

The grand prize was keeping Sean.

Our future with fewer responsibilities is finally here. Al and I have only one child to care for, but do we want to go to the movies and out to dinner, exercising our bitterly earned freedom? No, we want to stay at home by the fire, or cozy up in bed watching videos or reading books, and we want eight-year-old Hayley with us. We were doing what we wanted to all along, but I don't think we realized it.

I wish we had bought a larger bed when Sean was alive, so he could have lain between Al and I to watch late night television. Our double bed is cramped, and there was not enough room for all of us to lie down comfortably. We thought we could not afford a queen sized bed, but Al thinks we should get one now, before it is too late for Hayley as well. It seems redundant, though. I cannot bear to give Hayley anything that Sean didn't get to enjoy. I know that sounds warped, but I struggle with it.

Our local newspaper did another article about Sean and it was nicely done. They had done a feature when he returned to school after the relapse last year, and they wanted to do a follow-up after his death. We received cards and letters in response to the article from people we didn't know, as well as from people we did know. It was comforting.

Sean was also nominated for a Prudential Spirit of Community Award for the work he did in raising money last year for the Relay for Life cancer walk. Casey completed most of the paperwork for the nomination, and Sean's young principal, who is currently battling cancer himself, and his vice principal were excited about it. Al and I went to the junior high and spoke to the student council, and the local television station did a piece about Sean and the award. It was difficult to talk about Sean in public, especially when I would prefer to stay in this bubble I call home. The students and staff at O'Leary also want to create a landscaped memorial for Sean in front of the school.

I am grateful and deeply touched that they do not want to forget him. I didn't think it would be like this. I thought his memory would sadly fade away.

I baked chocolate chip cookies this morning, which I often did when Sean and Tyler were home, but who was I baking them for? Hayley does not particularly like sweets, and Al can only eat so many. I could eat the whole batch, of course, but that is another story. I found myself desperately hoping one of the boys would walk through the kitchen door, open the cookie jar, and cry, "Yes! Cookies!" Does that mean baking cookies for the boys was the pinnacle of my life and the rest is downhill, or at the very least uninspirational? Maybe so.

The *time heals* theory must be perpetrated by people who have not lost a child. Time heals only in the sense that you are eventually able to do the routine things you used to do, but it does not mean any of the pain lessens. I turn to ice when people try to reassure me with those words.

December 22, 1995

Tyler is home, and it's good to have him here. He was home at Thanksgiving too, but that seemed like an unhappy blur. I was thinking about the previous Thanksgiving, which we spent at Al's sister's house in a neighboring town, when Sean was sick and we stupidly didn't know what was happening. Tyler took his brother home early because Sean refused to eat any dinner, and Al and I kept glancing at each other with a wild panic. He was in remission, wasn't he? Surely the cancer had not returned already.

But two days later, we were on our way to Salt Lake City. Sean didn't have a kidney or urinary tract infection, as we had hoped. His cancer had returned, five months after the bone marrow transplant we hoped would save his life.

I asked Al which was worse for him, the beginning of the illness, when Sean was down to 89 pounds and too weak to stand up, or the relapse the following year. For him, the initial diagnosis was the lowest point. It was such a shock that something so awful could happen to our gentle Sean. But for me, it was the relapse. That put an end to my hopes and dreams.

SEAN

After moving to Salt Lake City for three months the previous summer, enduring the transplant, teaching our fragile son how to eat again, and worrying that when I returned to the bone marrow unit each morning Sean would be dead, I had significant hope that the transplant would give him more time. Five years, maybe, and that was somehow acceptable. It is odd how willing I was to accept the most pathetic compromises. Even if he could not be cured, I begged God to give Sean a few more years with us. Apparently, that was too much to ask.

For weeks after the relapse, I walked around with a hole in my heart. When people asked about Sean, I choked back tears. I tried to be cheerful around him, but even that became difficult. I grew more and more irritable with Tyler and Hayley, and I cried most of the time. In March, I began taking antidepressants, because I was fading away quickly and I knew I couldn't do that to Sean. The medication worked like a miracle, until after he died. Nothing seemed to work then.

When I saw the doctor last month, he said I was probably depressed and suggested trying antidepressants. Well, no shit, Columbo, but I have already tried Zoloft in varying dosages and it's not enough. I am on my own with this, and besides, I want to feel everything. Antidepressants mask your feelings and sometimes that is necessary, as it was when Sean was dying, but right now I need to *feel* all the pain.

There may come a time when I can't do that anymore, though. You can only stand so much grief before you snap into little pieces that no one can put back together again.

JANUARY

SEAN

It is life, life only, that sees death and comments upon it,
dreading the end of what it knows as itself and assuming,
through a colossal lack of imagination,
that what comes afterwards, if anything,
is as blank as that which it assumes came before.

—Alvaro Cardona–Hine

January 5, 1996

We made it through the holidays. On Christmas Eve, Al, Tyler, and Hayley went to Al's brother's house to see his family, who all live nearby. Last Christmas Eve, we invited them for dinner, as Sean wanted. The house was crowded and noisy, and it smelled like turkey and pumpkin pie. Though Sean's cancer had returned, we were so thankful he was still alive that we were able to put the pain behind us during the holidays.

Sean loved family get-togethers, but I could not face it this year. Whenever Sean's name is mentioned, Al's mom breaks down. She is struggling to stay afloat too, and I don't want to make it any harder for her by crying and spoiling Christmas Eve. The solitude at home was soothing, and I sat alone on the sofa in the darkened house, lit only by the Christmas tree lights and a slow burning flame in the fireplace. I talked to Sean as I often do, and I am certain he heard me. There were no miracles, no visitations, just a pleasant feeling that he was there.

Christmas morning, however, was strangely hollow. We got out of bed after seven o'clock (four a.m. used to be the norm) and finally had to wake Hayley. Al, Tyler, and I were subdued. I would not call it depressing, because Hayley was enjoying herself, but it was not like the happy Christmases of the past. We quietly opened presents, and Tyler said, "I miss sharing Christmas with Sean."

Tyler surprised me with a framed copy of John Lennon's drawing, *Beautiful Boy*. I didn't know it existed, so it was the best gift of Christmas for me. It reminds me of Sean, of course, and I am grateful that Tyler does not resent the attention I still need to give his brother. It was an unselfish gesture on his part.

We have started a new tradition. Each year we are going to hang a new angel decoration on the tree, date it, and mark the time that has passed since Sean's death. This year I put a white porcelain angel in his stocking. I hoped against all reasonable hope that during the night, Sean would take it out and put it on the tree so we would know he had been there. But I guess he is not going to indulge us.

When we were decorating the house for Christmas, Al suggested we hang Sean's stocking with the others, and when we did, we noticed it had an angel on it. Sean had chosen the stocking when he was a small boy, but we had taken the significance of the angel for granted and paid it little attention. Now it seems prophetic, especially when coupled with another discovery. When my mother was here a few weeks ago, we looked at Sean's baby quilt, the one she made for him when he was born. It is blue checked gingham, with embroidered footprints and triangular edging. Several embroidered figures are set in white blocks in the center of the quilt, but I had not realized that all the figures are child angels. I must have known this at some time, but I had forgotten. It seems like more than a coincidence. My sister finds it odd that our mother chose angels for Sean's quilt, because angels are usually meant for baby girls, not 'snips and snails' little boys like Sean. When Tyler was born, she made a cowboys and horses quilt for him. Why angels for Sean?

On a subconscious level, I think that some of us knew what was going to happen, that Sean would be a child angel too. Maybe life's answers are found within us. When Sean got sick, I knew from the very beginning that he was going to die. Sometimes (when he was doing well) I would reconsider, thinking I must be wrong and feeling relieved that I was. But I knew, deep down, that our little boy's days were numbered.

I remember sitting alone at the computer when Sean was in remission and attending school. That was a hopeful, rare time for us, but I was suddenly overcome with a deep melancholy and began to cry. A strong sense of forboding hounded me for days. Sean relapsed the following month.

Al reminds me that I used to predict, when I was feeling especially morbid, that one of our children would die young. I said this when they were still healthy and I tried to put it out of my mind, but the premonition continued to haunt me. Was it a normal mother's fear, or was it sent as a warning? I don't know, but the day we discovered Sean had relapsed after the bone marrow transplant, we took him to the local hospital for a scan of his kidneys, hoping his recurrent back pain was indicative of a pesky kidney infection. We were not overly worried at that point, because I had lulled myself into believing he was cured, but while I sat alone in the waiting room, I began to plan Sean's funeral. I cannot explain what came over me, but I was planning the service because somehow, deep in my heart, I knew it would happen. I had known it all along.

Five months later, when the numbness started in his chin last May, I was disconsolate. It took a long time for it to develop into something measurable, but I was convinced the numbness was bad news. I think Sean was too. He talked very little about death, but during the brief remission he wrote that prophetic poem. The last lines read:

"4 months go by, and you think you won't die,

then you get sick, it hits you like a brick.
The Cancer is there. They put you in bed
and now you dread the things that come.
You now feel numb, you think you will die.
Oh why, oh why? Now you are dead,
alone in your bed. The Cancer is dead."

It was always cancer with a capital C.

Sean left us another gift, evidence he knew more than he was letting on. The other day I was looking through his things and found the drawing pad he got last year for Christmas, along with a paint set containing oil pastel crayons, water colors, colored pencils, the works. He did not use the art supplies until later that spring, four months or so before he died, because he was far too ill to draw immediately after the relapse. He finished a few drawings during April and May, before the numbness and tumors in his head started growing at an unprecedented speed.

I must have seen the artwork before, because I was always interested in whatever Sean did, but I could not remember the drawings. Most of them were simple efforts at creating nature scenes, although one is different. It is colored with oil pastel crayons, and the setting is a green field with a river at the forefront and what looks like a yellow brick road running through it. The road leads to the back of the drawing where it meets up with a dense forest, mysteriously distant. A dark figure is standing at the edge of the forest, waving goodbye.

Al remembers watching Sean do that particular drawing in the hospital, but he had not paid attention to it either. Sean meant to leave this gift for us. It is one of the few things I know these days.

My sister sent a copy of something she read that comforts me when I study Sean's drawing. "Let us accustom ourselves to regard death as a form of life which we do not yet understand ...Death is but a departure into an unknown filled with wonderful promises." *(Maurice Maeterlinck)*

Euripides wrote, "How do we know that the dead are not living, and the living dead?" I like to think about this. It doesn't drive me crazy. It is the one thing that makes sense in a senseless world.

January 9, 1996

My friend Pam, a fellow schoolteacher for seven years, brought me a gift on Christmas Eve, a crystal figure of an angel representing my angel son. She also arranged a six pack of diet coke and a 2 pound package of peanut M & M's in a decorated basket. Pam knew I needed a fix, and she knows what my favorite fix is.

I was touched by something Casey's mom shared the last time I saw her. She said I had been an angel of a mother, but she was just being kind. I had an angel of a son, and I feel him with me nearly all the time.

January 13, 1996

We have had several family tragedies the past couple of years. Three months after Sean got sick, Al's 65 year old dad was diagnosed with pancreatic cancer. He was looking forward to retirement later that year so he could fish and camp more often, but he died a month after diagnosis. The night of Gene's death, we went to Al's mother's house to be with his two brothers and his older sister. Everyone was crying, yet Al and I could not. It was so strange, being unable to cry, but there was no emotion left. That is the only way I can explain it. We were sad, of course, but a father's death seemed more natural than what was happening to Sean. I suppose that sounds awful, but that is how things were.

After Sean relapsed the following year, my middle brother's wife was killed in a car accident. She was only 47 years old, and I clearly remember the phone call at 11 o'clock that night from my sister. "Julie, I hate to tell you this..." Mary's voice broke, and I knew it was something awful. At first I thought something had happened to my mom, but Mary said tearfully, "Christine was killed in a car accident tonight." I was so shocked I hung up on her. That time, oddly, I was able to cry. When I regained control, I telephoned Mary and she explained what had happened.

Chris and her younger sister were driving home to Northern Idaho from their parents' house in Pocatello (at the southern end of the state), because their father was diagnosed with prostate cancer and they were helping him determine what treatment to pursue. The two sisters were caught in a torrential rainstorm, not far from Christine's home in Sandpoint, which darkened the March sky at four o'clock in the afternoon. Both were wearing seat belts, but Chris passed a car and slid off the road, smashing into a pine tree.

"We made it, Chris!" her sister cried after the violent impact. She turned towards the driver's seat, but her older sister was dead. They had discussed death a couple of hours before the accident. "When I die," Christine had said prophetically, "I want it to be quick."

David's wife was a sweet, gentle person who never hurt anyone and whom people were drawn to because she made them feel good about themselves. Chris and David had raised three lovely daughters, and the last one moved out a few weeks before the tragedy. They were looking forward to having many years to enjoy the savings they had worked for during their marriage, with plans to travel, spend more time together, and enjoy their granddaughters. See what I mean about making plans? We set ourselves up for betrayal.

My youngest brother got the telephone call from the State Police, and he had to tell David, who had just arrived at his home near Boise for a visit. David drove his fist through the screen door, and he and his daughter, Mandy, took off immediately for Northern Idaho, where Christine lay dead in a morgue.

David is a reserved person, guarded with his emotions and very gutsy. But when Mary and I arrived in Sandpoint for the funeral, he met us at the door, sobbing. I had never seen him like that and it was heart wrenching. He was split open, and the core revealed a raw and tortured man. David and Chris had a wonderful marriage, and he will never find another person like her.

Three months later, when we were in California visiting my sister a few weeks before Sean died, my cousin Jeffrey (he was David's age) committed suicide. It made national news because he blew up the family home after poisoning himself with cyanide, and there were rumors of foul play and revenge surrounding his mysterious death. As children, my brothers and sister and I spent summers in the red roofed white farmhouse when my aunt and uncle were alive, and we all had a close connection to it. Their ancestral home, where my uncle was born, no longer exists.

SEAN

My cousin Laura, Jeffrey's younger sister, lives across the field from the house she grew up in. When she heard the explosion, she ran to the window and said, turning to her husband in horror, "He's finally done it."

Although I feel a great deal of empathy for my cousin - - that he was in so much pain the only alternative he felt he could act on was suicide - - Al responded differently. "Sean is fighting for his life," he said sardonically, "and your cousin just decides to end his."

Most people suffer from some level of anguish, however, that makes them question whether this life is worth living. My cousin came to his own conclusion. There are days I cannot argue with it.

A week later, Al's 18 year old nephew, Eric, was hit by a baseball during a game and it ruptured his liver. He spent weeks in Salt Lake City at Primary, and when he finally went home, he was not the same. He had suffered some brain damage, and now he has difficulty learning in certain areas, mathematics in particular. Eric related a dream he had at Primary, the same hospital Sean spent so many weeks in. Eric was critically ill when Sean was dying and his parents had decided not to tell him, because they didn't want to interfere with Eric's recovery. They were afraid their son was going to die too. In his dream, Eric was looking out the window of his room, down at the front entrance to the hospital. He saw Sean sitting on a bench by the loading area, waiting for someone to pick him up. After awakening, he asked his parents, "Is Sean dead?"

Sean warned us too. The day before his death, he slept heavily on the sofa, but had not entered a coma at that time. I was lying on the floor watching him, trying to read but unable to concentrate. Suddenly, he sat up out of a deep sleep and asked, "Am I going out–of–town today?"

"No," I replied, thinking he was confused. "You are

not going out-of-town."

Sean persisted. "Am I leaving the house today?" Again, I answered no.

He lay back down and softly said, "I thought I was going somewhere."

He didn't ask if *we* were leaving the house, he asked if *he* was leaving the house. At last I understood the impact of his words, and I watched him carefully the rest of the day and into the night. I was listening for the labored breathing, a signal that the end was imminent.

He died the following day.

January 15, 1996

I have been thinking about the horrors of the bone marrow transplant, which was done a year before Sean died. At first the insurance company would not approve a transplant, because they considered it experimental. BMT's had been done infrequently on rhabdomyosarcomas, and at the University of Utah Medical Center, they had attempted none on children with rhabdos. The transplant team recommended doing a peripheral stem cell transplant, using Sean's own bone marrow, something they typically do for patients with solid tumors rather than blood diseases like leukemia (which require a donor). After the BMT team at Primary and the university provided supporting information that a stem cell transplant would give Sean a significantly better chance of survival, it was finally approved. The new bone marrow unit was opening at Primary Children's, and Sean was the third patient admitted. Two older teens with leukemia were already there as donor bone marrow recipients.

Dr. O'Brien stated he was not certain a transplant would help Sean, but he knew it wouldn't hurt. In retrospect, I do not think the transplant was the best course of action for Sean, though I believe the doctors were acting in his best interests. I don't blame anyone for the BMT's failure, because Sean was a high-risk patient and his chances of recovery were not all that rosy from the outset. But the transplant team recommended it, and we left things to fate. Fate stepped in and decided to give our boy this opportunity.

My friend Melody recently reminded me that after I told her Sean was having the transplant, I added, "I do not think it is going to be successful." I had forgotten I said that, because on the surface I pretended that the stem cell transplant was his best chance of cure.

I have mixed feelings now. In one respect, I am glad we did it, so we don't have any more regrets about neglecting potential cures. But on the other hand, Sean was critically ill for several weeks during and after the transplant and the recovery consumed valuable time. I am not convinced the BMT extended his life either, because after he relapsed, his bone marrow had not fully recovered from the transplant and he could not be treated aggressively with chemotherapy. We sometimes had to wait six or more weeks between treatments, until the white blood cells recovered from the previous chemo. One month he had to have neupogen shots for thirty days in succession to get the white count back up to normal levels. It still didn't work very well, not after the transplant. The shots always hurt, even with the rotation of sites, and the neupogen burned on injection. Sean hated the whole process. The following month, I had a chat with his oncologist.

"Sean hates the G-CSF," I explained. "We will endure them for two weeks after each treatment, and if that is not enough to bring his counts up, chemo will just have to wait." His doctor agreed and we waited, but in the interim the cancer was able to take hold.

Bone marrow transplants can be a lifesaving opportunity, but it does not always work that way, especially with high-risk patients like Sean. People need to be aware of that. They also need to be warned about the difficult and frightening recovery period after the transplant, though nothing can really prepare you. It is something you have to live through to believe. But there was a blessing in the aftermath of the experience. Although I clearly remember what Sean suffered during the BMT and those memories come back to haunt me, Sean's recollections were dim.

"You know, Mom," he said a few months later, "I cannot remember very much about the time I spent in the transplant unit. But I know it wasn't good."

That was an understatement, and I thank God for his loss of memory.

We had two days notice before Sean was scheduled to check into the Utah hospital, and we left for Salt Lake City in the first week of May. The weekend before we left, Sean and Hayley went camping with Al at our land. Tyler and I stayed home, where I spent most of the weekend indulging in depression. I did not want to leave 6 year old Hayley, who had become very precious as the last child in our family, and all we would have left at home if Sean died. Hayley had another month of kindergarten before she could join us in Salt Lake. Al's mom worked in the afternoons and was able to take her to school each day, but I had to trust 17 year old Tyler, who drove his jeep like a typical reckless teen, to collect Hayley after school and return home safely.

105

I also worried about the hours they had to spend at home before Al returned each night, but Tyler was in charge and I had to trust him. The domestic front was out of my control. Sean was my first priority, and someone else had to step in and make sure my daughter was safe and secure, because I could not be there. Tyler did a good job, but I think Hayley was protected by a few angels, too.

I was afraid, mostly, of what might happen to Sean. We were walking into the unknown and the prospects were overwhelming. I cried and cried that weekend, and to make matters worse, the washing machine broke and gallons of water flowed out of the water lines, soaking our floors and carpets. Tyler took charge of the cleanup, because that last insult drove me to hysteria.

"Mom," he finally said patiently, "Sean is going down there to get well. Why are you crying?"

By the time they returned from camping on Sunday, I had mustered up the courage to face the immediate future. Sean's bravura was everpresent; he was intimidated by nothing. Why couldn't I be the same?

Sean and I left on Monday morning and spent the following two days undergoing a series of tests, including pulmonary function tests, CT scans, a bone scan, EKG's, blood tests. He had to drink 900 cc of the dreaded contrast before the scans, which helped the x-ray technicians see the areas they were scanning. Every time Sean had scans he had to suffer through drinking the contrast, plugging his nose and gagging with every sip. Once, he threw it all up and they had to put a tube in his nose and administer it that way. That was such an insult, and from then on he made valiant efforts to keep the liquid down.

They also did a bone marrow biopsy. The medical team wanted to make sure he was in full remission and able to handle the rigors of a transplant. The bone marrow biopsy was especially traumatic, though he had endured them before. A large needle is attached to a syringe and screwed into the lower back to withdraw a piece of bone and the adjacent marrow; all cancer patients have them done periodically. They also did an aspirate, taking out the spongy part of the bone marrow. Cell samples were studied under a microscope to determine whether there were any suspect or different looking cells which might indicate actively growing cancer.

Sean's bone marrow came out clean, in positive contrast to the results during the initial diagnosis, but the nurse practitioner who did the bilateral biopsy was not experienced and she had to insert the needle twice on each side. It was heartbreaking to watch Sean suffer. I sat beside him and let him squeeze my hand until my bones nearly cracked, but it did not ease the pain. He lay on his stomach, tears escaping through closed eyes, his face screwed up in contortions of agony when the needles plunged into his bone. It was a prelude of what was to come.

I rented an apartment the second day we were in Utah. The landlady, a young single mother, took pity on us and allowed a three month lease, though a six month agreement was required in most apartment complexes. We rented a charming little studio (cramped is a better word) with hardwood floors in a distinguished brick building called Scarsdale, only five minutes from the hospital. It was compact, with enough room for Sean and I, but far too crowded when Al and Hayley were there. During their weekend visits, we tried to stay out of the tiny apartment as much as possible.

I fixed it up, putting bedspreads, futons, pillows, and rugs on the credit card, trying to create a comfortable and cheerful atmosphere for Sean. He deserved that. We spent three weeks in our studio before his admission to the bone marrow unit, totally alone except for weekends when Al and Hayley came. I think Sean was happy to have me to himself. Later on, he said those were the best three weeks of his life. He and I did whatever we wanted, and we did it together, including lunches out, browsing in the mall and bookstore, and going to movies. We were best friends. I did some writing during the day while Sean read or played video games. One of his elementary school teachers had given him a book of challenging puzzles and mind games after his diagnosis, and he worked on it every day. Sean was a bright, clever boy and had a gift for mathematics that made mental exercises fun for him. I was not sharp enough to do them alone, but he helped me struggle through.

Chemotherapy followed the round of preliminary tests. Cytoxan, a chemotherapeutic drug that produces a significant number of stem cells during the recovery period, was administered in the hospital over a couple of days. The white blood cell count initially went down, when the chemo destroyed it, before it gradually built itself back up. When the counts reached a peak, Sean was scheduled to go to the university for stem cell collection.

He had another central line put in, using a surgical procedure similar to when he had the broviac placed in his chest. The new line was called a Davol, and it was twice the size of the broviac Hickman catheter. It was inserted, under anesthesia, on the other side of the chest through the jugular vein, by the same surgeon who had removed Sean's right testicle at the beginning of his illness. The line had to be large enough to facilitate the removal of the stem cells in a short period of time, so Sean would not have to stay in the hospital for days.

He was very uncomfortable after the surgery, because the Davol was placed in an awkward position and he could not rotate his head. For several days he walked around with his neck bent to one side in order to compensate. He hated the Davol and he hated having two central lines, which had to be kept dry and sterile. They were unwanted appendages, limiting him and reminding him of his vulnerability.

During the weeks following the Cytoxan treatments, we went to the oncology clinic at Primary for lab work three times weekly, where they monitored the white blood cell count. When it rose sharply at the end of May, stem cell collection began. It is similar to a blood transfusion, except that blood is taken *out* before being put into a centrifuge to separate regular blood cells from stem cells. Afterwards, the remainder of your blood is transfused back in. The stem cells were frozen and saved for rescue later on. Sean was at the university for four or five hours at a time, watching videos or playing games. It took four days to collect enough stem cells for the transplant.

He made a wonderful friend named Linda, a nurse in the apheresis unit. They developed an instant bond, and she visited Sean faithfully in the following months, sending gifts and letters too. When Sean relapsed, she visited him each night after work, and I usually took a break at that time. I learned that her little brother had died of cancer fifteen years earlier, which explained the connection she had with Sean. She continued to grieve over her brother's death. Time heals? Yeah, right.

After the stem cells were collected and the blood counts fully recovered, Sean was admitted to the new bone marrow unit at Primary Children's, where he lived in a sterile room for weeks. The BMT unit was an attractive facility with caring, competent staff, who tried to make our stay as easy for us as they could. I did not have to worry about leaving Sean at night. BMT nurses are in and out of their patients' rooms every five to fifteen minutes, because there is so much care involved with a transplant patient.

The first week was devoted to chemo, with a few rounds of the PANT protocol (an abbreviation for the kinds of drugs used to kill the cancer cells) which was extremely toxic and damaging to Sean. The purpose of stem cell rescue is to blast the system with enough chemotherapy to eradicate the cancer and the bone marrow as well. Left alone, the patient would die, because they are left with no immune system at all. But the frozen stem cells are brought in for rescue. After the new bone marrow *takes*, or engrafts, the patient is hopefully cured. It does not always work, though. The first patient admitted to the unit was a seventeen-year-old girl, and she died four months after her transplant.

Sean died a year later.

During the transplant, Sean was gravely ill. He quit eating almost immediately, vomited regularly for over a month, and all his bodily fluids were bloody. He required frequent platelet and occasional blood transfusions. He became so ill, he could not watch television, play video games, or tolerate any noise. Dr. Petersen, on several occasions, said Sean was about as sick as they got.

For several days when he was battling intense fevers, I laid next to Sean on the hospital bed and literally held him down because he was shaking, nearly convulsing. It was terrifying. I had to leave him alone at night because I had Hayley during that time, but the nurses were extremely vigilant and that eased my fears to some degree. Hayley and I spent twelve hours a day at the hospital, and she entertained herself by reading, drawing, and acting out plays. When Al came on weekends, someone was with Sean for 16 to 18 hours a day, and that was better.

Whenever Al was with Sean, he was *really* there. He devoted all his time to taking care of Sean's needs, and by the weekends I was burned out and needed a break.

Hayley did too. She wanted to be in Salt Lake with me, but it was a difficult situation, and we often left the hospital in tears when Sean had a particularly bad day. Hayley was always afraid her brother was going to die, and he was so cranky, which he had a right to be. She whispered instead of talked, and could not watch television because Sean had no tolerance for noise. Everything we did irritated him.

Hayley entertained herself by quietly reading most of the day. The positive side of the confinement was that her reading skills were advanced for her age. By the time she entered first grade, she was tackling difficult books and understanding the content.

After the stem cells were transfused (a bone marrow transplant is simply a transfusion) it was nearly two weeks before Sean began to improve. Before engraftment occurred, I often wondered if he would leave the hospital alive. There were endless days of sadness and despair over what he was going through. The only thing that kept me going was the hope of a cure. The weekends were better, when Al came to visit and Hayley and I had a break from the hospital routine. I was always anxious to get out of there, but I feel guilty about that now. Sean could not leave. He was imprisoned in the hospital, and I just waltzed out and went to the mall or out to eat.

It was desperately unfair.

Tyler visited twice, and my mother came for a week to help with Hayley. The complicated network of tubes connected to Sean frightened her. She was afraid of saying the wrong thing and so she said nothing at all, but Sean understood her fears. He knew she loved and adored him, as Al's mom did. My cousin Laura and her two daughters visited, as well as Dr. Adrian's family, his nurse, and a friend of Sean's from Twin Falls. But Sean was too sick to talk to them.

111

SEAN

As he began to feel a bit better, he started getting out of bed, walking around, and even taking baths again. When bathing, Sean couldn't be allowed in the bathroom alone, and he didn't want a nurse sitting with him while he was naked and all, so I did the honors. I turned my back to him and sat in the room while he bathed, just in case he slipped and fell. It was a quiet, private time, because we knew no one would bother us in there. He shared some of his feelings and once said, "Mom, most mothers and sons don't have a relationship like ours. We're really lucky." I remember feeling decidedly *unlucky* as he said that, but I murmured something encouraging, that yes, we were very fortunate, but I was thinking the opposite. I was thinking that I would give up my wonderful relationship with Sean if he didn't have to be sick. But of course it doesn't work like that, and now I know that he was right. I was really lucky; the luckiest mom in the world to have a son like Sean.

When he was released from the hospital, after spending a month in isolation, we stayed a couple of weeks at an old friend's house, who used to own Sean and Tyler's preschool. They offered us their enormous, rather elegant home, because they were out of town most of that particular summer. It was located directly across from Primary and had a pool, which was great fun for Hayley. Sean liked it there, especially after being confined to a small hospital room.

Sean was unable to eat or drink in the transplant unit and had lost the desire. Nothing sounded good, so he had to relearn normal eating habits before returning to Idaho. In the meantime, we fed him with intravenous supplements through his davol line. He was psychologically motivated to eat, but it was difficult. The mere mention of food made him gag.

It was a major milestone when Sean drank his first

soda, the day Casey came to visit from Twin Falls. Casey's parents took Hayley to the zoo, and Casey stayed at the house to visit. Sean was not eating yet, but we took them to a restaurant and Sean pretended to eat a taco. It was a beginning.

We began making daily jaunts to fast food restaurants for milkshakes and baked potatoes with cheese, fries and fry sauce, anything to tempt Sean's flagging appetite. Sometimes he would eat only one bite, but we had to keep trying. After he learned to eat again, we returned home and had a family get–together to celebrate. My cousin and her daughters, my mom, my sister Mary and her kids came to Twin Falls. Sean was in his glory. He had been to hell and made it back. We had a cake made that read "Welcome Back, Sean."

He spent the rest of that summer at home and at our land, recovering and resting. In retrospect it was a pleasant time, compared to the horrors of June and July. When I drove back to Salt Lake City to clean out the apartment, though, I cried the entire time. I could not forget the anxious, sleepless nights I had spent there, lying on the futon, tormented by the constant, nagging fear that Sean would die during the night without me at his side.

I had a dream during that time in which Sean was in a hospital room, dying. I burst out of the room and ran into the hallway, pleading with his doctor, "Can't you do something for him?"

"There is nothing more we can do," the doctor had answered grimly.

I returned to Sean's room, all alone, and held him while he slipped away. Was it just a dream, or was it a foretelling of the future?

SEAN

January 28, 1996

I love this house. It is my refuge, and Sean's memory is preserved within these walls. While he was sick, we sat in the living room and watched nature through the wall of windows looking out on our version of beauty, the high desert of Idaho. We spotted rock chucks hiding in the rock wall outlining our tiny lawn, the occasional deer maneuvering its way through oversized sagebrush, and our favorite porcupine nesting in a Russian olive tree. The neighbors shot him this year because he was eating the bark off of one of their trees. I do not understand people anymore.

Now I sit on Sean's threadbare sofa upstairs, the one he died on, and stare out the Palladian window, trying to catch a glimpse of the nearby canyon and Shoshone Falls, as he used to do. When I walk down the stairs, I imagine Sean navigating them late at night when he was nauseated. He would lean, ghost like, against our bedroom doorway and whisper, "Mom, I'm sick."

He did not want to wake his dad and sister, but I was always half–awake, always listening for Sean. I would follow him back upstairs and lay down on the carpeted floor outside the bathroom, where he would retch into the toilet, again and again. Sometimes he would let me touch him on the shoulder, but mostly he just needed someone to be there.

Right now, I need this house. I need its memories to console me—and sometimes, to hurt me.

January 30, 1996

I am revising my book (this is the *third* unpublished mystery novel) and feeling proud that I have been able to stick with it day in and day out with a new resolve. I feel like I have to. I feel driven to write, but I no longer see the point in writing books about people killing each other and that is what mysteries are all about. I cannot seem to find a new focus, though, so I suppose I'll continue on this path until I do. At least I'm trying to work, so things must be slightly better than they were last fall, when I could not do anything on a regular basis. But the pain and sorrow are constant. I saw Casey the other night, and he confided that none of his friends understand what it is like for him. He will be in a good mood, sailing along, and boom! A dark cloud descends and he cannot control it. I confessed that I felt things were even worse - - the pain of missing Sean, that is. "I know!" he cried, eager to share his grief. "I thought it would be better now, but it feels worse."

It may never get any better, at least for Al and me. "Julie," Al said the other night, "this may be as good as it gets. We will probably feel like this for the rest of our lives." His comment surprised me, because he is usually upbeat, but I am afraid he is right. This is the way it is; this is what we are left with.

Hayley and Tyler have been affected by their brother's death in subtle ways that other people would not notice. When I telephone Tyler unexpectedly in the middle of the week, for instance, he asks worriedly, "What is wrong? Did something happen?" We are all waiting for the other shoe to drop.

Hayley sleeps on a futon in our room every night. She is frightened, terrified actually, to sleep alone upstairs. When Sean slept in the bedroom opposite her own after

SEAN

Tyler left for Colorado, she was all right, but now it is different. Al thinks she is afraid because she saw Sean die on the upstairs sofa. I suppose that may be part of it, but I think she does not want to be separated from us. She refuses to spend the night at a friend's house, and she used to think that was great fun. Hayley still likes the *idea* of sleepovers, but when she attempts to go through with it, I get a telephone call around midnight from a tearful child who wants to come home. When Al is late getting home from work, she panics. "Do you think Daddy is okay? Do you think something bad happened?"

Our children's sense of security, of trusting their parents to take care of them, is gone.

I experience feelings of intense despair and I have no control over the duration. When Super Bowl Sunday arrived, we made plans to do the usual family thing, eating pizza and downing a six pack of soda while watching the game. Al and I were not enthusiastic about continuing the tradition this year, as we have lost part of our family, but I insisted we make an attempt. I was feeling proud of my strength and drove into town to pick up the pizza, after stopping at a gas station to get a fountain diet soda, my drug of choice. The friendly clerk commented on my refillable cup with Utah Jazz signatures, which Sean got at the hospital. Sean loved the Jazz. The clerk began talking about her friend who has a twelve-year-old son who loves the Utah Jazz too. She decorated his room with Jazz memorabilia, and I heard about it in detail. By the time I returned to the car, I was really depressed. Listening to a simple story about a mother who did something nice for her son (that I could not do) ruined my whole week.

I went to the cemetery and cried on Sean's headstone.

20

January 31, 1996

My mother is visiting my sister in California. On the plane trip from Boise to Sacramento, she was sitting next to a woman who was about twenty years younger than my mom, who is 76. They had not said anything to each other because my mother was thinking about Sean. My mom is a very sensitive person, and apparently the woman sitting next to her noticed that she was upset. She asked my mother what was troubling her, and Mom told her about Sean, that he had recently died and she could not cope with it. Her traveling companion paused and said, "I would like to share something with you, if I may."

She told the story of her own son who had accidentally died as a teenager. After his death, the woman was destitute for months, then years, and the grief was undiminished. One day she was doing the dishes and crying buckets of tears into the sink full of water. Suddenly, she felt someone hugging her from behind, and she spun around, surprised because she thought she was alone in the house.

It was her dead son. He spoke to her without hesitation.

"Mother, do you know how hard you are making it for me? I need to move on. I have a lot to do, but I cannot do it until you allow me to." He faded away as suddenly as he had appeared. His mother had a strong feeling that her son was all right and not grieving for his life on earth, and that he wanted to continue his eternal progression.

Although the woman confessed that she still grieves for her lost son, the experience
has helped. "If my son is all right," she offered kindly, "your grandson must be too."

What a coincidence that my mom happened to sit next to a woman who offered a powerful personal experience that helped her cope with the grief. Or was it a coincidence? What are the chances of that happening on a random basis?

We had an experience of our own, something concrete. A couple of weeks ago, on a Friday night, we went to the high school basketball game and returned home late. One of our angel pictures was lying on the hardwood floor. We have three angel prints, framed reproductions of old world paintings which hang on the two sided brick fireplace. A pair of Victorian angels hang on one side, and around the corner is a Renaissance angel holding a trumpet. The framed Renaissance angel was on the floor, four feet away from where it should have fallen, upright and unbroken. No one was in the house while we were gone, so who made it fall? Did it fall by itself?

We experimented several times with a similar sized frame, without the glass in, but it always fell directly below the brick wall. If the print had fallen by itself, the glass would have shattered when it hit the hard floor. Secondly, it would not have slid four feet across the floor and around a corner, backwards, to land at the bottom of the stairway by the front door. That picture would have needed legs to manage that stunt. Al and I looked at each other and grinned. Simultaneously, we came to the conclusion that Sean had been here, though we know it sounds pretty far-fetched.

I was exuberant for days. The following Friday night (after another basketball game) we found the second angel picture lying on the carpet, where it had fallen off the brick above the fireplace mantle. It was also lying four feet away, next to the piano bench, upright and unbroken. This framed print slid four feet across the *carpet*.

We know it was Sean. He created the mischief, with a gleam in his bright eyes and a sly grin, to let us know he is still around. If it was indeed him, I am certain the third

"Sean was here—"

picture will soon fall.

SEAN

Sean

Sean, during Chemotherapy

The Quilt

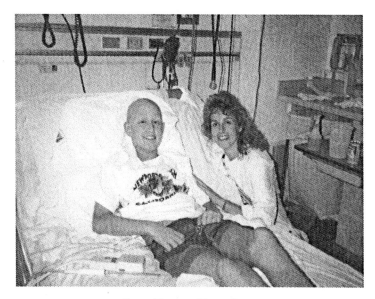

Bone Marrow Transplant

Relapse

Christmas

14th Birthday Party

SEAN

"Relay For Life"

Sean, a month before his death

FEBRUARY

SEAN

Some seek God in Mecca,
Some seek God in Benares.
Each finds his own path
and the focus of his worship.

A River Sutra
—Gita Mehta

February 6, 1996

The third angel picture fell, just like the others. I had returned home from a walk, and I found it lying on the floor, unbroken and upright. Sean has been here. I cannot tell anyone, though, outside of those who are close to me, because no one would believe it. But that doesn't matter anymore. Al and I *do* believe, and that is enough. Sean is trying to comfort us. He is so close, much closer than we thought.

February 10, 1996

I am a different person now. The changes in me would not be obvious to anyone else, but I know I have changed. It has taken months for things to settle, and I am feeling more at peace now. Everything happens for a reason, and some day I will understand. It suddenly seems okay to wait. It is all right when we don't get everything we want in this life. When things fail to go as planned, it can work to our advantage, because we begin to understand ourselves and our motivations. Knowledge and love are all we can take with us to the next world.

If everyone believed in an afterlife, that our existence is eternal, would that be enough to change the world? If

127

we knew we had to get along with others because we were going to be with them for all eternity, would we make more of an effort to accept individual diversity and avoid hateful conflict? If we understood we had an eternity to live, would we be less interested in getting exactly what we want, *right now*, and perhaps make loving and caring choices that would have eternal benefit for us and for those we love? I think most of us would, because we could examine our frustrations, prejudices, and hatreds differently. Trying to find meaning in this life is an incredible test of character, though, and as soon as you begin to understand something, it is difficult to hang on to it.

I think Sean is all right. But I wonder if he wants to come back and be with us, if he longs for us too. Does he feel as Beth did in the film version of *Little Women*, when she was dying and said, "But I know I shall be homesick for you, even in heaven."

I remember something Sean conveyed the night I felt his presence back in October. I asked him if he missed us, and he hesitated before communicating that it was a different kind of longing than ours. Perhaps Sean meant that he understood why we had to be apart and it was not sorrowful for him. Al believes Sean is content now. He compared our boy's suffering here on earth to what it is like for a woman to have a baby. The end result is wondrous, but the process hurts. It is not something you want to repeat.

I do feel changed, and I am looking at things a bit differently. Melody telephoned yesterday, and I was able to tell her about something I had struggled with for years. Best friends in childhood, we had grown apart for several years, and even now, when I make the hour drive to visit her in Hailey, I have trouble with my own feelings of loss and disappointment over unrealized dreams. Her busy life spent rearing seven healthy and happy children is full, and my life seems empty in comparison. But I am learning to manage those feelings, and they are not controlling me anymore.

When Sean got sick, Melody tried to renew our friendship, which had long been distant. She continued calling and did nice things for Sean, giving him a T-shirt, photo, and baseball cap signed by Arnold Schwarzenegger, and a baseball signed by Bruce Willis. She offered to lend me money for Sean's treatment. She did not give up, though I was characteristically distant, as I am with most people. At last I understood that she had loved me since we were children, and that perhaps I could be her friend again.

We were close when Al and I lived in Japan. Melody visited, and the two of us traveled by ferry to Korea for an adventure (I was five months pregnant). When I turned 16, she gave me a beautiful hardback copy of *Gone With The Wind*. She knew how much I loved books, especially that one. Now I wonder if the separation was largely my fault.

I admit to being envious of her life; she was a stay at home mom with seven kids, and that is what I had always wanted. I wanted her life and I could not have it. I had to finish college, and working full time was essential, because we didn't have enough money to live on. For years, it was easier for me to stay away. Now I am truly happy Melody's life has turned out the way it has, and I appreciate her setting me straight on the *imperfect* aspects of her life. Meeting the demands of seven children leaves her with no time for herself, the struggle with supporting that many children is constant, and everything is more complicated. But I admire the way she has raised her children in the face of social criticism, as few people approve of large families these days.

SEAN

It is all right that my life didn't turn out the way hers did. I was not meant for the life she is living, even though that was what I thought I wanted. It is a relief to admit I was envious, but the envy is gone now. I can accept that she does some things better than I do. Melody admitted she was envious of me as well, and afraid she couldn't talk to me because I had been in school for so long and prepared for two careers. Tongue in cheek, I reminded her that I am currently unemployed. We laughed about how silly we were.

We can't have everything, and though I did not get *exactly* what I wanted, I have gotten a great deal. I have a supportive, caring, passionate husband with whom I am more deeply in love than the day I married him, and three great kids. My personal life has been blessed, and I have learned from the disappointments, especially from the tragedy of Sean's death. I am almost grateful for the insight - - at least for today— because I am free of my past way of thinking.

My perception of the world was grossly flawed, and I seldom saw things as they really were.

February 14, 1996

When something wonderful comes along, I am always afraid something bad will happen to equalize the good fortune. When Tyler was accepted into the Air Force Academy last April, Sean and I were really excited. Sean had confidence in Tyler all along, but he made an interesting observation. "Well," he said jokingly, "now that this has happened, I will probably end up in the hospital for a month." We laughed about his dire prediction, but it turned out to be true. Tyler got the opportunity for a wonderful education and that was a great blessing, but it was balanced out, far on the negative side, with Sean's death three months later.

I have incorporated some fresh philosophies in my life, and though they have been around for centuries, they are new to me as I begin to channel them into my existence. I believe all our previous life experiences and the knowledge of our own future are stored in our brain, the part we cannot tap into. Sometimes this knowledge slips out and warns or enlightens us. That is why we need to practice listening to our hearts, because the answers to our lives are found deep within us. Even when no one agrees with your decisions, you have to stick by what you believe is right for you, like I did when I married Al and as I am doing with my writing, though it remains a long shot at best. Sometimes our decisions fail to turn out the way we hope they will, but I would rather make my own mistakes and not someone else's.

I thought this philosophy had emerged out of nowhere, but it is based on Plato's "Teutonic Model of Knowledge", written 300 some odd years ago B.C. So much for virgin knowledge.

February 15, 1996

I have suffered from nightmares over the past few weeks, tragic dramas about everyone close to me dying. I dreamed that Tyler was killed in a car accident and Hayley was hit by a car. I stood on a hill, unable to move, as I looked down at Hayley's motionless body lying on the road. I remember thinking that if Hayley was supposed to die, there was nothing I could do to stop it. I also dreamed that Casey died and I spoke at his funeral. I had two separate dreams in which Al died—once in a car accident and once from cancer. These are not psychic dreams, because there are too many of them. I am simply obsessed with death and afraid of losing anyone else.

February 16, 1996

I feel calm today, like Sean is following me around. Last night I had a magical experience, so sacred I can hardly put it into words for fear of contaminating it.

As I was drifting off to sleep, I had a vision of Sean, but it was not a typical dream because I was not asleep. I was in some kind of altered state, in between sleep and wakefulness, fully aware of what was going on around me. I was lying in bed on my side, facing the wall and struggling to fall asleep, as I do every night. Al, who falls asleep when his head hits the pillow, was sleeping soundly on the other side of the bed. Suddenly, I opened my eyes and Sean was standing right next to me. He was smiling and all lit up, and I reached out my hand to his. The room was completely dark, but I could see him clearly, so he must have been illuminated. He was wearing an ivory colored gown and he grinned broadly, as if he had a beautiful secret. I felt a strong physical impression, something I have never experienced in a regular dream. A burning in my heart, an overwhelming impression of warmth, permeated my entire body but was especially strong in my chest.

The burning sensation, I believe, was an assurance that Sean was really there, that I was not imagining it. Sean communicated without words that he wasn't just watching over me, he was *right beside me.*

February 19, 1996

Al and I talk freely about Sean now, and I am happy about that. The other night Al relayed some of his own fears and regrets about whether we did the right thing for Sean, with him working all the time so we could keep up with our bills.

"You have always been responsible," I said. "You were bound to do the responsible thing."

"Yes," he answered sadly, "but was it right for Sean?" I gently pointed out that whenever I suggested he take some time off, he got angry and defensive. "I know," he said despondently.

But I wasn't perfect either. I have already written about that. My feelings of isolation and fear during Sean's illness escalated into bitterness towards Al, and I knew I needed to step out of that. I have, and Sean is helping me now, encouraging me to love more. We hold back love, like we are saving it for something, but what are we saving it for? Love is not like a bank account, where we hide our money so no one else can take it. Love should be freely given, but most of us can't do it.

No one can get all the love they need from a fellow human being—we are not capable of giving that much. Our love is immature. But I know Sean is getting all the love he needs now, and the best thing I can do for him is to love his dad. Sean does not want to be responsible for a family breakdown. That would make him sad.

February 21, 1996

During the brief remission following the bone marrow transplant, we had a few scares, particularly during the month of August. Sean began having right thigh pain, and since this mimicked his original symptoms, we were concerned. After several trips to Salt Lake City for CT scans, bone scans, and MRI's that showed nothing unusual, we finally visited a neurologist and an orthopedic physician at Primary. The orthopedist identified the problem as myralgia (inflammation of a nerve) and cured it with a single shot of steroids. The first scare was easily resolved.

Sean had the 100 day bone marrow checkup in mid-September and the broviac was removed, after the BMT team pronounced him cancer free. We knew the next year would be critical, but we optimistically hoped for a long remission. Sean and Tyler flew to California to see my sister and her family because their cousin, Patrick, was going to live in New Zealand for a couple of years. Sean did fairly well for the first few days, but he returned home ill. He had the usual trouble with vomiting and I assured Mary, when she telephoned each night of the visit, that this was nothing extraordinary. But it *was* unsettling. The struggle with nausea and vomiting never ended, and his physicians had no explanation.

Sean returned to school at the end of September and

attended full time until Thanksgiving. Most mornings he woke up nauseated, but he went to school anyway, reminding himself that he always felt better after a couple of hours. He had excellent teachers, kind and sympathetic. At parent-teacher conferences in early November, Holly, his English teacher, said Sean had transformed her unmotivated fourth period class. When Sean came into the room, he sat down and began working. Everyone watched him and followed his example. Holly and Kelly, his reading teacher, were Sean's stalwart friends in the following months. When he became too ill to attend school, they brought food, gifts, balloons, and cards to the house, reassuring Sean that he was missed and needed. When I consulted with the team of teachers after Sean's cancer had returned, Mr. Asay, his big, strong history teacher, cried. I was touched by their compassion.

Sean's young principal, Wiley Dobbs, was currently finishing treatment for Hodgkins disease at the time, so they had a lot in common. A few months after Sean's diagnosis, Wiley was diagnosed with cancer. We saw him shortly afterwards in the treatment room at our local cancer center, where Sean was receiving a blood transfusion.

"Isn't this ironic?" he said with a hint of a smile. We discussed the humiliation of the disease and agreed that he and Sean had acquired all the "character" they needed. They did not need the cancer to give them any more. Wiley sent notes periodically, encouraging Sean in his battle.

Sean continued to have problems with vomiting during the remission, but everything else seemed normal. We finally accepted it as part of the healing process, and Dr. Adrian prescribed Zantac for possible ulcers. I wonder if Sean was ever in full remission. Perhaps the microscopic cancer cells were hiding, gathering strength for the next attack. At the outset we were told that the cells you cannot see are the most dangerous; they are the ones that kill. The bone marrow transplant had destroyed most of them, but not the strongest, most resilient. They were waiting for another chance.

Sean underwent physical therapy that fall and hoped to play eighth grade basketball in January. The coach was determined to get Sean on the team, even if he was not physically ready, and I appreciated his optimism and acceptance of our son. "The other kids still view Sean as a great athlete," he offered encouragingly. But Sean had experienced neurological damage from the medication Vincristine during the initial phase of treatment, and his balance and strength were vastly compromised.

It warmed our hearts, however, to meet new people who loved our boy and wanted to help him regain his former life. Sean played in a three-on-three basketball tournament at the beginning of November, and he and his buddies placed second. It was difficult for him to move with any speed, but he had a good time. His athletic friends, rather than complaining that Sean was keeping them down, appeared happy to have him participate and let him shoot the ball whenever he wanted. His friends on the other teams were indulgent as well, and congratulated him when he made a basket. It was all pretty laid back, unlike the competitive athletic events of the past. But we did not realize how monumental Sean's participation was. Al and I were always exhausted, it seemed, and we left the tournament early, missing Sean's last organized ball game.

We still had a lot to learn in the following months. Al says we hadn't *gotten* it yet, not at that point. After a couple of months of remission, we were pretending everything was normal again. "The next time someone in the family gets a terminal disease," Al offered sarcastically the other day, "we will know what to do." Hindsight creates its own set of problems. By the time you have things figured out, it is too late to do anything about them— except feel guilty.

In mid-November, Sean began having problems. One Friday night he stayed over at a friend's house, but came home early in the morning after throwing up most of the night. He tried to telephone, but we did not hear the phone. He began having trouble urinating, and I suspected a bladder infection. We visited Dr. Adrian's office, had blood drawn, and sent a urine sample to the lab. Our doctor said bladder infections were highly unusual for boys, and though the lab results showed blood in the urine, there was no infection. Sean began taking antibiotics because we could not think of anything else to do, but he didn't improve. We telephoned Dr. Trotter early the next week (the Adrians were out of town for the Thanksgiving holidays) to continue the medication.

The onset of intense back pain was a warning signal that something was seriously wrong. He had some mild pain off and on through November, but had not complained about it. By Thanksgiving day the pain had worsened and he was obviously ill. After consulting with the pediatrician on call at the hospital, I felt certain it was a kidney infection; the back pain corroborated my instincts, and kidney infections were among the acceptable realm of possibilities. That was something we could deal with.

We went to our local hospital for a CT scan of the abdomen, and the results were not good. I had to drag the specifics out of the doctor, though. He came to the waiting room as Sean was getting dressed and announced that the kidney was obstructed. Al and I glanced at each other in relief. A kidney obstruction could surely be fixed, we were both thinking. But it quickly dawned on me that the doctor meant to say more; he was simply not brave enough to find the words. No one wants to be the bearer of more bad news. I looked up at him and asked in a small voice,

SEAN

"Are we talking about a possible obstruction by another tumor?"

He nodded his head and said, "Yes. You need to return to Primary Children's."

"Can we wait until tomorrow?" The weather was not good and I was worried about travelling at night.

"It cannot wait," he said urgently.

Salt Lake City was encased in snow, white and frozen, symbolizing the current mood of our family. Our luck had gone from bad to worse. I questioned the doctors at the hospital that holiday weekend in detail. I dogged the residents, who were kind and informative. I studied the scans and listened to their theories, hoping against hope that my knowledge of Sean's disease could cure it. Dr. Bruggers was on call that weekend, and she and Dr. Snow, a urologist, consulted with a radiologist to place a stint in Sean's ureter where a probable tumor was creating a blockage into the kidney. The procedure was a nightmare.

The radiologist placed an external drainage tube, which was internalized several days later. Sean was sedated for the procedure, but they did not put him under. Al and I waited outside the procedure room, listening to Sean cry out in pain as they threaded the stint through the urethra, bladder, and into the ureter. The doctors confidently assured us that Sean would have no memory of the discomfort, but we could hardly believe them, judging from the anguished cries in the adjoining room.

The complete procedure took three hours. Dr. Snow and Dr. Bruggers tried to console us, but there was nothing to be consoled by. Our oncologist had been painfully honest. It was impossible to determine Sean's response to a new round of chemo, especially since he had already received the ultimate treatment: a bone marrow transplant. We did not know how far the cancer had spread, or even if it *was* definitely a malignant tumor around the ureter. A surgery was scheduled for mid–week to remove, excise, or identify the mass, though they believed it was a recurrence of the rhabdo.

The stint relieved Sean's back pain by the next day, but new problems surfaced. Urination was painful and very bloody. Sean was cranky and out of sorts, the stint hurt, and Al had returned home to work for a couple of days. I was left to deal with the uncertainty of what was happening to our son and to consult with doctors over future plans. Sean wanted me to stay with him all the time, of course, as I was his only thread of security. I returned to Ronald McDonald House late each night and cried myself to sleep.

I had a particularly bad night on Monday. I was terrified of losing Sean and could not bear the thought of going on without him. I suddenly understood what it would be like if he died, and the feelings of despair were more than I could bear. I cried continuously into the early morning hours and fervently prayed for some kind of help, though I had not been particularly religious for years. When I woke up the next morning, my sorrow was magically lifted. I was filled with a palpable, warm sensation of comfort. I could almost touch it. This new feeling assured me everything would be all right, that what was happening to Sean was not an accident. I had an overwhelming awareness that Sean's future had been planned and carefully orchestrated. I walked around the hospital with a sensation of warmth surrounding me for the next couple of days. It didn't evaporate until Thursday, the day the surgery was scheduled.

An oncologist had done a bone marrow aspirate on Monday and it was clean, free of cancer. They had not scheduled any more CT scans, though, and I felt cautiously optimistic that the tumor was isolated and thus easier to eradicate. Dr. Matlak, who had removed the testicle when Sean was initially diagnosed, was scheduled to do the surgery. Matlak is a business like man, but he was kind to Sean and later told Dr. Virshup, whom we were meeting for the first time, "Sean is a great kid, you know, really exceptional."

Dr. Virshup, the attending oncologist, ordered a chest CT for Thursday, before the surgery. He was not satisfied with the minimum of tests and felt we needed more extensive screening. I agreed. Al returned on Thursday, just in case the CT scans or surgery revealed the worst, but the surgery had been delayed and we didn't know why. As Al and I stood outside Sean's room that evening and watched the team of doctors filing down the hall towards us, I knew it was the worst of news. Dr. Matlak and his assistant were accompanied by Dr. Virshup. The CT, we were informed, showed new tumors in the chest, behind the right lung. They could not recommend performing the surgery for the sake of a diagnosis, especially since Sean was weak and thin, having plummeted down to 90 pounds. The rhabdo had clearly returned. I held my hand up to stop them and ran down the hall, crying, away from their terrifying honesty. Al was left to discuss the details, because I had reached the end of my rope. Our fears had come true. The comfort was gone and I was left with emptiness.

A couple of days before Sean returned home, Al and I took him out of the hospital for an hour or two. His nurse was more than willing to help us with the escape, but the doctor said he could not give official permission for the outing. "Insurance companies have a problem with that sort of thing," he explained, "but I agree Sean needs to get away. I just cannot give you *permission*," he said, winking.

We put Sean into a wheelchair and went for a ride in

our van, planning to take him to the Festival of Trees downtown. But he didn't feel up to that. Instead, he wanted to have lunch at an Italian restaurant. He barely ate anything, but we visited and made plans for Christmas, and Sean began to feel human again. I wish we had done that sort of thing more often. I wish we had taken the trouble to find out what Sean wanted. He never demanded anything for himself. That was not his way.

After spending another week in the hospital, we returned home. By the time Christmas rolled around, Sean was feeling happier and a little stronger. I took photographs of him before he lost his hair again, because after the remission he had grown beautiful, thick brown curls and I hated to see them go. But the photos are very sad. When we forget how bad it was for Sean, we look at those pictures and see that our skeletal boy, with huge, haunted eyes, looked like a holocaust victim.

I was afraid the chemo wouldn't work its magic the second time around, so I gave Sean a video game and a pair of silk boxer shorts as early Christmas gifts. I was thinking with trepidation about the teenaged girl who was in the transplant unit when Sean was. She made it to the 100 day mark, relapsed, and died three weeks later. With a jolt, I realized time was growing shorter and could be up at any moment. It sent me into a panic.

But Sean grew stronger gradually, though he was not well enough to return to school until February. He had difficulty keeping anything down. Pills were definitely out and food only marginally in. He had cumulative nerve damage from the Vincristine he had received during the initial treatment phase, and he had difficulty walking; it was easy to trip and fall and that humiliated him. After the stint was placed in the ureter to the kidney, he urinated frequently and was unable to wait for more than half an hour without a trip to the bathroom, which created more challenges at school. The teachers bent over backwards to accommodate him, but Sean was embarrassed. There was a new problem as well: nighttime enuresis. He had to wear pads in his underwear, and it was a major indignity, though only Al and I knew about it. Hayley had trouble with bedwetting too, ever since her brother had become ill. "Now both of us are wetting the bed," Sean pointed out soberly, "and I am thirteen years old." That broke my heart, and there was nothing I could do except try to convince Sean it was not a big deal, that other people suffered from incontinence, people without cancer. But he was skeptical and frustrated. He gradually adjusted to the loss of his dignity, though, and was eventually able to joke about it.

During the hospital stays, Sean needed intravenous Ativan to calm him down so he could sleep. On each admission, he would tell the nurse practitioner what drugs he wanted and she would smile and oblige him, because his requests were generally reasonable. It gave him some power, and in the hospital he could not sleep without medication. When he and I travelled to Salt Lake alone, I typically left late at night and returned early the next morning, because I was unable to sleep in his room. My energy reserves were so low, I had to be selfish on that point. One morning I walked in and saw a fresh faced Sean, who appeared surprisingly well rested. "How did you do last night?" I asked.

"Well," Sean replied, grinning broadly. "That Ativan must have done *something*, because when I woke up this morning, my Attends was on the floor and I was buck naked!" We laughed over that—a lot. It eased the humiliation. When he was in the hospital, they loaded him down with IV fluids and the ativan made him sleep heavily, so Attends were necessary because the incontinence was worse than usual. On one occasion, when we arrived at Primary for a three day stay, Sean said with resignation, "I guess it's back to those damned diapers again!"

The first set of scans showed reduction in tumor size, so that was good news. Dr. Virshup pointed out Sean's tremendous response to chemo the first time around, and argued that there was no reason he could not enter a second remission. Finally, someone with a positive word. We seized on his optimism and tentatively began planning a trip to Hawaii when Sean entered his second remission, the next fall, possibly. But we were overly optimistic, and it was particularly interesting that Sean was not eager to make any long range plans after his relapse. He didn't sink into full scale depression, but he did not want to talk about the future. He began living for the moment, and eventually, so did we.

By February he was having significant problems with back and left shoulder pain. The doctors feared the cancer had spread to the liver, but scans denied that possibility. It was finally determined that the extensive bone involvement from the cancerous cells had deteriorated the spinal column, so that the vertebral fractures he had at the beginning of treatment had worsened. Sean's bones were rubbing against each other as they gave way. In effect, his spinal column was slowly collapsing. He could not sit for long periods, and standing up sharply increased the pain. We talked about using a wheelchair, but Sean refused. We finally let it go, still hoping he would take a turn for the better.

The tumors did not diminish during the following months, but at least they had not grown. I told myself I would not get upset until they showed a significant increase in size, but the standstill was disturbing. In April, Dr. Snow removed the stint, believing the tumor surrounding the ureter was now outside of it. Sean was overjoyed. We interpreted this as good news, but sadly, it was short-lived. When we returned to Salt Lake a month later, the kidney was extremely dilated and the tumor was not any smaller, as they had hoped. Sean had another surgery and the stint was replaced. It was the beginning of the end.

February 22, 1996

On Monday I cried a lot, convincing myself I was not going to get through this. I considered going back on the antidepressants, but they dull every little emotion and I want to experience my feelings, even when they are unbearable. At the end of the day I felt slightly better, although I was unable to sleep that night. I laid in bed thinking about Sean and what kind of future I could possibly have.

The following morning I returned home from a walk and sat alone on the sofa, thinking about how long it had been since we heard from Sean. I was feeling hopeful and started talking to him, like he was right beside me. "Talk to me, Sean," I pleaded. "Come on, talk to me. I need to hear from you." I sat on the sofa for quite a while, but nothing happened. It never does when I ask for it, so I went upstairs and worked on the computer. An hour later the telephone rang, but no one was on the other end. I have answered several of these mysterious telephone calls over the past few months, and wondered whether they were simply wrong numbers or, more strangely, some contact from Sean. That seemed unlikely, so I tried to ignore my feelings. I never received more than one call a day, though, and they were always spaced several days apart. They sound like long distance communications, and after several seconds the line goes dead. I hung up the telephone receiver and returned to my writing. An hour later it rang again, the same as before. These calls had never come so close together. I tried not to think about it; surely it was my imagination. Al came home that afternoon, and I tentatively shared my suspicions. He did not make any judgments and we decided to pay more attention to these telephone calls and see what happened. After Hayley returned from school, I was working alone in the kitchen when the phone rang.

No one was on the other end. I stayed on the line a few moments before hanging up, but that time I knew it was Sean. My knees were weak and my hands trembled, but in a good way, like I had been visited by the gods. I remembered what I had said that morning. "Talk to me, Sean." When Al got home that night, he knew something was up, and when I told him what had happened, he said it was probably our boy, letting us know he was still around. If it *was* Sean, I thought, he would probably call one more time, just to convince us skeptics.

We were all in the kitchen when the phone rang a few minutes later. Hayley answered. "Hello?" she said again and again into the receiver. Al and I stared at each other, then at Hayley. She unaware of what had happened earlier, but when I anxiously grabbed the receiver, it ended just like the other calls had.

We feel blessed. Why are we being allowed this frequent contact? I do not know, but it is a great comfort. Besides, I think other grieving parents may have had similar experiences, but who is going to talk about it and risk being ridiculed? I read that 75% of all parents whose children die see them in a vision or a dream within the first year of their deaths. A lot of us are not talking, because we are afraid no one will believe us. We can hardly believe ourselves. Skepticism contaminates our experiences, so we keep quiet.

February 24, 1996

About 9:00 this morning I received a telephone call exactly like those I wrote about in the previous entry. I stared at the telephone after I hung up for a long time. When Al called a couple of hours later, I asked him if he had phoned earlier. "No," he said slowly. "Did you get another call?" I admitted that I had, but added, "I refuse to get excited about a single telephone call."

We laughed nervously and ended our conversation. I walked away from the kitchen and into the bathroom, where my hot bath water was waiting. The telephone rang again. I raced back to the kitchen and answered it. It was the same type of call—Sean's method of communication. This time I stayed on the line and told Sean how much I loved him without words. The call lasted longer than usual, and after I had expressed my love for him the line went dead. Was Sean answering my denial of the earlier call's significance? Was he trying to say, with a mischievous grin, "Oh yeah, Mom? Well, listen to this."

This has lightened my gloomy mood, and I welcome any relief.

February 26, 1996

I desperately want to change my life. The old life has faded away, and I do not want my future to resemble the past. I am not sure I can teach again, certainly not at the school where I taught when Sean and Tyler were home. The boys spent a lot of precious time with me at Bickel Elementary, an old brick building with drafty ceilings and cavernous halls. After school they would help me correct papers at the miniature first grade tables and we would share a soda, or sometimes they would just stop by to say hello. It always made my day, because I never had enough time with either of them. Returning to that atmosphere would be painful for me.

I don't want to be in the same place in ten years, because the old lifestyle is not working anymore. I need a change. I love this house deeply, but sometimes I want to fly away. The months pass, though, and I am still in the same place, so I guess that is wishful thinking. I cannot run away from this. There is nowhere to go, and realistically, I have no money to run away with. I am stuck in my past and there does not seem to be a future.

Sometimes the guilt and regret machine kicks in, and I think of everything I missed out on when the boys were growing up. I was in college or working all the time, and much of their childhood passed by in a frenzied haze. I was unable to take them to school and seldom picked them up; they rode the bus and walked the mile from the highway to our house. They came home to an empty house, and we are probably lucky they didn't get abducted on the trek home. I was concerned for their safety but felt powerless to change things. I had to work. I was totally devoted to them after work hours, though. At four o'clock every day, I was on my way home. I had no social life, and we did nothing without the kids. When I was not working, I was with them. I wanted to be; that was the least they deserved.

The year before Sean got sick, when he was in the 6th grade, I tried to pick him up once or twice a week and bring him back to school with me. The need to be with him was suddenly overwhelming. Sean demanded very little from either of his parents, and sometimes he got pushed into the background because he was such an easy child. At bedtime, I used to climb the ladder to Sean's top bunk and lay beside him for a few private moments before he went to sleep so we could discuss his day. Otherwise, he got little attention. Our other children were loud and assertive, bless their hearts, but Sean was satisfied with leftover scraps. It breaks my heart to think of how little he demanded.

When I drive Hayley to school now, I often linger in the idling car as she walks into the building. I am struck with a sense of wonder, like I am watching something precious, something that will never be repeated. The ritual has become dear, and I want to hold onto it. I suffered from tunnel vision in the past, though. When Tyler was a senior in high school, Sean was home most of the time, and Tyler was finished with classes at 2:00 each day. He needed no extra courses to graduate, and he did not want to assume an academic load that wasn't absolutely necessary. This attitude annoyed me, because I firmly believed Tyler should be using his free time productively, studying or exercising—doing *something* worthwhile.

The senior year began as I feared. For half the year Tyler was not involved in after school sports, so he came home at two o'clock every day and played video games with Sean or watched television with him. With considerable irritation, I informed Tyler that this was simply not going to work. I have always been afraid that our oldest son would be lazy, that his work ethics were blatantly unamerican, and I tried to shame him out of it. He responded by staying at school longer, and I think he was a little hurt that I didn't want to spend time with him as well. But I refused to see it that way, because I was seeing only what I wanted to see. Al gently pointed out that perhaps Tyler wanted to be with his mom and brother, and if he was spending time with Sean, that was certainly worthwhile.

Of course it was, I finally learned, but that time is gone and I wish I had appreciated it more. The American emphasis on productivity and *being the best you can be* is not all it's cracked up to be. Sometimes it causes us to alienate ourselves from our children when we suspect they are unmotivated and undisciplined, which we assume will lead to disaster. But was I seeing things correctly? Was Tyler unmotivated, or did he want to spend more time with his family? Personal relationships are far more important than how many facts are crammed into your brain. *Love* is more important.

Tyler's time at home was a gift, especially as the hours with Sean slowly dwindled away.

February 27, 1996

I always worried about leaving Sean in the hospital overnight, so I would telephone the nurses' desk at 1 a.m. and sometimes at 4 to confirm that Sean was okay. But there were a few vigilant nurses I trusted. Rick was one of them, Sean's primary care nurse in the bone marrow unit. Late one night, Al and Sean were watching television when Rick came in to adjust the IV. Sean was extremely groggy from drugs and watching a pizza commercial advertising *buffalo wings*, a marketing name for barbecued chicken pieces.

Sean stared sleepily at the television and said, as if it made perfect sense, "I didn't know buffaloes had wings."

Rick got a real charge out of that, and he and Al grinned at each other, struggling not to laugh. It was the cutest thing; an especially sweet memory that I continue to cherish.

"Sean was here—"

MARCH

SEAN

Dark angels follow me
Over a godless sea
Mountains of endless falling
For all my days remaining.

Why Should I Cry For You?
—Sting

March 10, 1996

During one hospital stay, Sean and I watched a lengthy news report on gang violence. "Mom," Sean said sadly, "they don't know how precious their lives are, do they? They just do not understand." He said this without judgment; he was simply making a statement about what he had observed. Most of us cannot comprehend that our actions have an eternal impact. This life is incredibly important.

I have had only one of those strange telephone calls since February. It took Sean weeks to convince me it was him. Finally he had to go overboard, making four calls in one day and two the next, in direct response to my pleas for comfort. I did get a genuine wrong number the other day, but it was completely different from Sean's calls.

March 12, 1996

Sean's application for the Prudential Spirit of Community Award went to the state level, but I did not think he would win. Last week we were notified that he is the middle school winner for Idaho, and they are sending us to Washington, D.C. to accept the award. It is just like Sean to give us much more than we can ever give him.

There is some irony to this, though. Sean was always entering one contest or another, but he never won anything. He finally wins an award, and he's not here to receive it! I think he'd get a good laugh out of that.

He will receive a $1,000 memorial, and we are donating it to the American Cancer Society's "Relay for Life," on O'Leary Junior High School's behalf. Last year the relay was held two months before Sean died. The students at O'Leary raised $5,000, and Sean was the prime motivating factor. I do not think he realized it, but his classmates cared about him deeply. Across the top of the fundraising posters they wrote, "WE LOVE SEAN."

Sean was excited about the cancer walk, though I shamefully admit I had trouble mustering up much enthusiasm. After two years of living through the high drama of cancer treatment, I was almost reduced to zombie–like behavior, going through the motions but too exhausted to care.

Sean and Wiley Dobbs, his young principal, planned to walk the survivor's lap together, but Sean had to walk slowly because of back pain. He ended up walking and chatting with Char Davis, a friend and medical social worker at our local hospital. She has been in remission from cancer for over twenty years, and Sean loved her jokes and cheerful attitude. A couple of weeks before he died, Char came to the house and talked to Sean in private, with kindness and honesty, about him going on ahead of the rest of us. It broke the tension, and after that Sean began talking more freely—with me, anyway. His impending death was no longer a secret. It was finally out there.

Holly and Kelly stayed with Sean the night of the cancer walk, which was held at a football stadium. It was Hailey Hodges' birthday, one of Sean's close friends (she read his poem at the funeral) and afterwards they went to her house for a party. It was a great night for Sean, his last night among a group of peers. Earlier he had fallen down on the bleachers, and the fall made a huge black and blue goosebump on his knee. Kelly was horrified, but Sean offhandedly assured her it was nothing, that those things happened all the time. That was hardly true, but he desperately wanted people around him to be relaxed and happy. He did not want them to focus on his fragile physical condition.

We all went to the relay, Tyler included, and the master of ceremonies introduced the cancer survivors at the onset. Tyler soberly pointed out the obvious. Sean was the only survivor who was not in remission, though he cheerfully informed the announcer that he would be soon. Sean's optimism was always hard at work.

March 14, 1996

I am reading a lot, but different books than I used to. I have already read scores of British mysteries, and I find my tastes roaming in other directions these days. Colin Dexter's Inspector Morse always lures me back, though. He is just as reserved and unfriendly as I can be, and he often gives up his bad habits—for an hour or two, and then forgets he ever made such resolutions. I am not interested in reading about someone who has a handle on things. How could I identify?

I recently read *An Anthropologist on Mars* by the author of *Awakenings*, which explores in five separate scenarios how people with extraordinary handicaps adjust to what the rest of us consider tragic circumstances. One scenario involves a blind man whose sight is restored when he is an adult. He had always interpreted the world without vision, and when he finally sees with his eyes, it turns his secure and sightless world upside down. Having his vision restored was not the blessing it was supposed to be.

Al's brother, the baby of the family, is in a wheelchair. Skip was struck with a mysterious disease called Transverse Myelitis when he was 19 years old. The disease made him a paraplegic overnight, and 13 years later, his life is an example of courage and perserverance. He has developed a wonderful sense of humor, has a steady job, and he married a secure woman who is willing to deal with the challenges of having a handicapped husband because she loves him. Actually, he does not allow the chair to limit him and neither does his wife, Deanna. He often pokes fun at his handicap; he tells a story about travelling outside Yellowstone Park and having a serious accident on his four-wheeler. The paramedics took him to the nearest emergency room, where he was released several hours later. The following day he and Deanna were planning a float trip on a nearby river, something his wife was really looking forward to. The accident threatened to ruin those plans. The next morning, Skip was lying on a bed in a motel room, sore and scraped, and looking forward to resting up from his accident. His wife, Deanna, jumped out of bed and cheerfully announced, "Up and at 'em. Float trip today!"

Skip groaned and said, in as pitiful a voice as he could muster, "Deanna, I'm really hurt. I can't do it." But Deanna was not about to let him bail out on the float trip, so after some bantering back and forth, they finally bandaged him up (Skip claims he looked like a mummy) and went on the float trip— that day. Skip lives a very full life. I doubt I would be that courageous.

I want to change the way I have looked at things for

the first 37 years of my life. My outlook was not completely faulty, but certainly one dimensional, like the frog that sees straight ahead and has no peripheral vision, thus experiencing a limited view of the world. Limitless, untapped knowledge and power exists within our universe, but we are unable to comprehend. Egotism is our greatest barrier. How can we presumptuously assume we know everything about our purpose on earth?

Twentieth century human beings are afraid of their spirituality. We have created a world afraid of life and death, full of violence and disrespect. Many people are living lives without purpose because they think it ends with their physical death. They do not feel any responsibility for their actions, so they hurt people and do what they like.

Al and I taught our children responsibility and respect for others, but I am sorry I did not encourage spirituality as an integral part of their lives. Everyone has to find their own way to God, and though religion can provide spiritual salvation for many people, it fails to make sense for others. I am one of those lost souls who is uncomfortable with formal religion, but God is omnipresent and He does not confine himself to churches, temples, or synagogues. There are many different ways and places in which to reach Him. Do not give up the search for spirituality because you are unable to find it in traditional avenues. You will have to create your own path.

March 16, 1996

My brother David recently shared something that is similar to the experience I had with Sean. The week after David's wife died in a car accident, their three daughters and granddaughters were staying the weekend at his house. The oldest granddaughter, Meghan, slept upstairs with her baby sister in the guest bedroom. The following morning, three–year–old Meghan came down to breakfast and brightly announced, "Grandma Chris was here last night. She was all lit up, and Grandma Olive was with her." Olive was Meghan's great–great–grandmother who died when Meghan was a baby. How did this three-year-old child know it was her?

The night Sean appeared at my bedside, he was "lit up" too. No one can convince me it did not happen, but some people might describe the visitation as *wishful* thinking, that I willed Sean to appear in an attempt to deal with my grief. But if I were wishing for a mystical experience, I would not have wished for that one. I would want Sean to be on the living room sofa, for instance, and have a long conversation with real words. I would hear his voice. I would hug him, and the interaction would be much fuller.

I did not wish him up. Besides, whenever I desperately want to dream about Sean, I am unable to. I do not have the power to induce visions.

The junior high school has been raising money to build a landscaped memorial for Sean, in front of the offices and entryway. Al and I have been attending committee meetings of students and staff, and the group finally decided on a fairly expensive project. We will need $5,000 to complete it. I am already nervous about spending so much money, but Wiley has insisted on making Sean's memorial something to be proud of. Contributions are trickling in, and the students are raising money every which way they can think of. Some of the contributions have come from people we do not know, and they are very generous. One of the first donations was for $1,000, from a family whose sons were friends of Sean and Tyler. We are overwhelmed by their generosity. They wanted to remain anonymous and also offered to cover any shortage at the end of the fundraising drive. I hope that will not be necessary, but their selflessness is exemplary.

There has been another change in me. I have been unable to speak publicly for nearly twenty years, but I was able to address the student council at O'Leary on two brief occasions. For someone who has a near phobia of being on stage in public, it was a major accomplishment. Last week I spoke at the high school basketball recognition night, because we awarded a scholarship in Sean's memory. I was afraid I would have an emotional breakdown and make a total mess of it, and whenever I contemplate speaking in front of a group of adults I go crazy with fear. But the last time I was calm, strangely so. I was not speaking to the United Nations, of course, and the fate of the world was not hanging on my words, but it was a huge milestone.

The compulsion to change is coming from outside myself. I love feeding into my fears, but someone is encouraging me to overcome them. Even if the changes are only minor, I am grateful I'm not the person I used to be. My innocence is gone, life will never be the same again, and oddly enough, some of that is a blessing. I want to be open to the mysteries of life and death and continually change my perception of the world I live in. I do not want to know all the answers—not right now. People who think they *do* know it all are deluding themselves. Surprises are in store for all of us.

One belief remains constant, however. The spirit world is close. Sean has simply stepped into another dimension, and that is why he's aware of what is going on in our lives. With high tech innovations like virtual reality at our fingertips, it should be easier for a person living in the late twentieth century to accept that theory. Sean is nearby, living in another dimension.

When he died, he stepped through an invisible door.

March 20, 1996

I do not know how a mother can grieve so much for one child. I don't know what to do with all this pain. It is eating me up, and the memories of Sean's suffering really hurt. I am not asking why he had to die, but why did he have to suffer again and again? Whenever it seemed like he reached the limits of endurance, the anguish persisted. I wish I had done more to make it better. I am so sorry, Sean. I wonder if you know how loved you are and that nothing can take your place. My sadness continues to grow, with no end in sight. I feel truly alone in this world. No one understands.

I am a stranger here.

March 22, 1996

We watched a news segment about the American boy who was murdered in Italy last year. The seven–year–old child was visiting Italy with his family, sightseeing and travelling by car. They were exploring ancient ruins in the countryside, and the boy noticed a dove landing in the ruins where he and his mother were standing. His mother explained that doves, historically speaking, are messengers from God. Shortly afterwards, the small boy was shot by Italian thieves. Was the presence of the dove coincidental? Absolutely not.

When I heard this family's story some months ago, I decided to have an etching of a dove carved on Sean's headstone, because he was our messenger from God. The recent television news story did a follow–up on what had happened since the little boy's tragic death. After their son was murdered, his parents decided to donate his organs, in spite of their shock and grief. This was significant to several Italians who were recipients of the organs, because they got a second chance at life. The boy's father was interviewed on television, and I was deeply impressed and touched by his reaction to the tragedy. He was very calm and expressed no anger towards his son's murderers, but the sadness and bewilderment were obvious. He gravely pointed out that no one wins in a situation like that, because he and his wife will suffer over the loss of their son for the rest of their lives, and the families of the murderers will suffer as well for the actions of their children.

These parents had the courage to turn their son's violent death into something good. Their gift has had an extraordinary spiritual impact on the people of Italy, as well as the rest of the world. In America, lawsuits would have been considered first. We are a greedy bunch of money grabbers, and when tragedies occur, we want to make sure someone pays. I doubt that really helps. I do not know if turning the other cheek helps either, but I suspect that those who can adopt this attitude gain more spiritual peace.

I am amazed at how these American parents handled their son's horrifying death—with dignity, grace, and benevolence.

I am also interested in the power of goodness and the "domino effect." Unselfish acts seem to spread and influence others, and it happened when Sean was dying. When Melody's husband was building Sean's casket, he went to the lumberyard to buy the pine. The co–owner of the business asked him what he was building. When he explained, the man offered to donate all the lumber. The next day, Melody and her husband came to Twin Falls and brought a pizza for Sean from his favorite restaurant in Ketchum. Melody had asked the owner to make a special pizza because it was for a special reason. They responded by writing a kind note to Sean and refused to let Melody pay for the pizza. This may seem like a small thing, but to us, it was important.

March 25, 1996

Al is not a grief therapist, but lately he has been counseling a number of clients who have lost children. Previous to Sean's death, Al was a cerebral and nonmystical man for the most part. Now he is seeing things a bit differently. He bravely began asking his clients who had lost children the following question: "Did anything unusual happen before or after your child's death?"

I do not know who his clients are and I do not want to know, because their identities are confidential, but their experiences support our own. Nearly everyone Al counseled reported that they had seen their child or had some premonition of their death. One client was grieving over her murdered son, and when asked if anything strange had happened since his death, she replied without hesitation, "Yes. I have seen him on two occasions."

In the visitations, her son assured her that he was all right and that everything would be okay. These experiences have helped the woman resolve certain things, but the grief remains. Healing this kind of pain is not that simple.

She also shared a premonition that took place before his death. A week before he died, she had a disturbing dream on the eve of a sporting event he was planning to participate in. During the dream, he was violently killed (the details were unclear) and flung against a fence post. The following morning she shared her concerns with her husband and tried to talk her son out of participating in the event. No one paid her any attention, but oddly, the particular event was cancelled. A week later, however, her son was murdered outside a convenience store.

His body was found leaning against a fence post.

If death is merely random and accidental, why did this mother have a premonition of her son's death, especially when he had not been ill and a violent end could not have been logically foreseen?

Another client lost a son in a car accident. The boy was a football star at his high school and had told his mother, hours before his death, that he didn't think he would be able to finish the current athletic season. Surprised, his mother wanted to know why, but he had no explanation. It was just a feeling, the boy claimed.

He was killed that evening.

Again, if death is a random event, why was this young man warned of his seemingly accidental death?

One of the most moving experiences shared with Al came from the mother of a suicide victim. She claimed to have seen her son twice after his death, but the circumstances of dealing with a suicide were so tragic that she could hardly talk about it without crying. One night she was lying on her bed, struggling to fall asleep, when she opened her eyes to see someone standing at the foot of her bed. It was a tall, angelic man dressed in white robes, and somehow she knew it was Jesus. She sat up in bed and asked, "Where is my son? I want to see him."

The angel stepped aside and she saw that her son, dressed in regular clothing, was standing a few feet behind him. He hung his head, refusing to look at his mother, and he was crying. There was no other communication on that occasion, but a few weeks later she again saw the angel, or Jesus, appear at the foot of her bed. She asked him the same questions, and he stepped aside to reveal her son standing behind him. The young man was standing closer to the angel and he was not crying anymore, but he still refused to look at his mother. This time, however, he was wearing a white robe.

For the parents of suicide victims, this is a great comfort. If you accept the woman's experience, it is clear that God is helping this young man to resolve the pain that caused him to take his own life. Undoubtedly there was shame involved, because the son would not look at his mother, but clearly, progress was ongoing.

I am not the only one who has seen my dead child and witnessed evidence of his continued existence. Perhaps the experience is more universal than we think.

March 30, 1996

We finished the work on Sean's landscaped memorial. The trees and bushes are planted. A few kids and staff at O'Leary energetically helped complete the project, and Al, Hayley, Tyler, and I were there too. Pavers were arranged in a circular shape, and three curved, stone benches are surrounded by bushes and trees, some of which are bermed and covered with bark. Two bronze plaques are set in stone in between the benches. The smaller plaque has Sean's name and date of birth and death. I tried to find a brief quotation for the other plaque, but the verse his friends chose was the most appropriate. It is a quote from the 1994 film, *The Shawshank Redemption*:

"Some birds aren't meant to be caged;
their feathers are just too bright.
And when they fly away,
the part of you that knows
it was a sin to lock them up does rejoice.

But still, the world is that much more
sad and empty now that they're gone.
I guess I just miss my friend."

We are very fortunate. My sister has a close friend who lost two children, one in an auto accident and one to suicide. No one created a public memorial for her kids. Parents usually grieve in private for their forgotten children. We are blessed in this respect.

We took some of Sean's friends out to lunch afterwards. I am relieved it is done, but a dedication to the memorial is planned for May 20th. Wiley wants me to find a speaker for the service. But who?

SEAN

"Sean was here—"

APRIL

SEAN

Our friend and we were invited abroad...
His chair was ready first, and he is gone
 before us. We could not all conveniently
start together; and why should you and I be
grieved at this, since we are soon to follow,
and know where to find him.

—Benjamin Franklin

April 4, 1996

A year ago Sean was still alive. He was feeling much better than after the relapse, so we were guardedly hopeful and decided to go to Disneyland for a few days. The new Indiana Jones ride was opening, and Sean wanted to see what it was like, but I think I wanted him to go more than he did. He obliged me, though. Tyler was Disneylanded out, so the four of us travelled alone, which simplified the sleeping arrangements. Sean had to have his own bed. We went at the beginning of May and were gone for four days, but the brief trip was hard on Sean. There was a considerable difference in his energy level compared to the previous year. The Disneyland trip Wishing Star gave him a few months after the diagnosis was the best family vacation we had ever had. Everyone was agreeable and exceptionally caring about Sean's needs. Tyler and Hayley grew weary of their brother's illness later on, and became tired of catering to him, but at that point they had not worn down yet.

We took things much slower on the second trip, which we charged on the credit card. The first day Sean complained of jaw pain and numbness in his chin. We pumped him with painkillers, and I desperately prayed he would be allowed those precious four days before entering a crisis. We enjoyed ourselves for the most part, but a couple of nasty Disney employees on the Indiana Jones ride cast a pall on an otherwise pleasant experience. One employee asked why Sean could not wait in line for two hours like everyone else. I told her about his fragile condition, but she responded coldly, "He has cancer, so that means he can't wait in line?"

I struggled to maintain control of my emotions and not embarrass Sean, but she definitely needed a good slap to wake her up. Her cruel comments were disappointing and made Sean feel that nobody cared about him but us.

I have to chalk it up to ignorance. She reminded me of the nurse who examined Sean in the emergency room just before his diagnosis. I had sped three hours to Salt Lake City on the freeway while Sean vomited continuously, because Dr. Adrian thought I could get there faster than an ambulance. By the time we arrived at Primary Children's Hospital, Sean was so weak he could not sit up and his blood calcium was dangerously high. I tried to convince the nurse that he needed a bed immediately and was unable to wait any longer in the waiting room.

"Oh yeah," she said icily, "every mother thinks her child is sicker than anyone else's."

Well, I know that Sean was the sickest kid in the emergency room that night. Again, I have to chalk it up to ignorance. She didn't know any better.

We were allowed that final trip to Disneyland, and after returning home we drove back to Salt Lake for more chemotherapy and to find an explanation for the numbness. A head CT scan was done but nothing definitive showed up. There was a fuzzy spot in Sean's skull, however, which had appeared in the previous scan. We visited our dentist at home and had full x-rays done, but the jaw pain and numbness were not dental problems. Since my sister had recently recovered from a six-week bout with an infected tooth and osteomyelitis, with similar symptoms, I wondered if Sean had the same thing.

Dr. Lemons, an oncologist at Primary, said the fuzzy

place in Sean's skull was inconclusive. He also cautioned us that it was too early to tell, but that later on we might realize it was advancing disease. We waited with trepidation. The numbness came and went, but it always returned and was sometimes accompanied by low-grade fevers. Sean took antibiotics, which helped intermittently, but his jaw often hurt and on one occasion became grossly swollen.

We were driving home from our local hospital after a blood transfusion in mid-May, and Sean was studying himself in the car mirror. "There's something weird about my head, Mom," he pointed out. I agreed and promptly called the nurse practitioner at Primary to discuss this strange phenomenon. It was as if Sean's skull had shifted, or perhaps it was the swelling that made it appear that way. His bald head had previously been smooth, but all of a sudden these randomly distributed bumps appeared on his skull, and they had not been there the day before. The swollen areas popped out of nowhere, disfiguring his scalp and making Sean appear somewhat alien. The nurse practioner was puzzled, and oddly enough, by the next day Sean's skull was back to normal. Now I know, and knowledge always seems to come too late, that there were significant changes occurring in his head all along, but it took several weeks for it to develop into something visible.

I bought airline tickets to Northern California, where Mary and her family live, because Sean really wanted to go. At first he refused to visit his cousins until the kidney stint was removed and the nighttime enuresis resolved, but he finally adjusted to the probability that this was not going to happen. He adapted and readapted, over and over. Sean must have felt like no one listened to what he wanted, especially God.

Tyler was leaving for the Air Force Academy in Colorado at the end of June, so the week with my sister was a last hurrah—literally. Sean's condition was unstable, and I worried that he would not get the trip, that we had already asked for too much. But he rallied and was able to go.

Sean informed me that all he wanted to do in Stockton was visit with his cousins—no sightseeing, please. That was fine with me. I spent time with Mary, and the kids played board games, video games, and ate plates of nachos. Mary still thinks of Sean whenever she sees a can of nacho cheese.

We took the kids to the movies one day, but the film Sean wanted to see was sold out. He was not feeling very good, but he didn't complain about going, in typical Sean fashion. When we learned the movie was sold out, he sighed with relief and mumbled, "I'm so glad." Bless his heart. He made himself go because he thought everyone else wanted to.

We visited the Sacramento Zoo. Mary's husband got a wheelchair for Sean, and a family outing sounded like fun to our weary boy. We stopped at the mall to eat lunch on the way home, and Sean ate a huge piece of pizza and a gyro. "Sean," Uncle Sid cautioned, "you're going to be sick, you know."

Sean smiled and said, "Yeah, but it sure tastes good now."

He did throw up that night, but for him, it was well worth it. Sean wanted to feel like a normal teenager for a few hours, and now I am grateful that we refused to put severe restrictions on his activities. We let him do whatever he wanted, even when his blood counts were low, though he was usually sensible about what he could handle. As it turned out, overprotecting him would not have helped him live any longer. It would have robbed him of the opportunity to have friends and feel like any other kid, on the rare days he was allowed to.

The weekend after returning home, we drove up to our land and stayed for the day. Al had bought Sean a new four-wheeler for his second birthday, which he was looking forward to. The second birthday was the date of the bone marrow transplant, June 13th, and it was supposed to commemorate a cancer survivor's rebirth and date of cure. Sean was not cured, of course, and we knew he would never have that second birthday. But he continued to talk about it, even after the relapse, and I had to stop myself from pointing out the obvious, that there had been no cure.

Finally I acquired a few brains, and we decided to give him another birthday anyway. The four–wheeler we gave him and made payments on was well worth it, though he rode it only a few times. When Al was debating whether to purchase an expensive, unnecessary vehicle we could not possibly pay cash for, I pointed out that he would never regret anything he did for Sean. We only regret the things we did not do.

After riding the four–wheeler in the mountains one day, Sean woke up with a painful stiff neck. His bones were so weak, he could not handle the weight of the helmet. When Al got home that evening, after working on the cabin over the weekend, he suggested we drive to Louie's Italian Restaurant in Ketchum for dinner, an hour and a half away. In spite of Sean's discomfort and the fact that he could not turn his head at all, he was determined to enjoy dinner with the family. It didn't matter how his body felt; his spirit was determined to enjoy life. I did not think the excursion was a good idea, but I am so glad we went. It was Sean's last dinner in a restaurant.

In retrospect, his life and death seemed to be carefully planned, but by someone else. I wanted him to have the trips to Disneyland and Northern California. I hoped Tyler would finish basic training at the Academy before Sean approached the end. Even his death happened on an auspicious day, right before the weekend, allowing family and friends to get there in time for the funeral. Holly said matter-of-factly, "Sean was just trying to make it convenient for everyone. He always tried to do that."

Two days before Tyler left for Colorado, I took Sean to see Dr. Adrian. A couple of growths had appeared on the back of his skull while we were visiting my sister in California. Sean claimed that he had bumped his head and I tried not to worry, but the bumps seemed to be growing. We had an x-ray done, and Bart telephoned us later that day with the results.

The bumps showed up as holes in the skull and were highly indicative of metastasis. Sean's cancer was on the move again.

We returned to Primary the day Tyler left for Colorado. After a course of Thiotepa, a third line drug used when everything else has failed, the bumps continued to grow. We measured the growths before leaving the oncology clinic, and I continued to measure them after returning home. They kept growing, so I finally stopped. Sean knew they were larger, though, and he wanted verification. I wanted to lie to him, but I could not. He deserved better than evasions and subterfuge from the person he had always trusted with his life. Instead, I began talking about death.

He raised his hand to stop me, like he was directing traffic. "I *know* Mom," he said tearfully. "I know what is going to happen."

I am glad I opened the lines of communication, though I was not sure I was doing the right thing. During the last couple weeks of his life, Sean was able to talk about his impending death. If he had not felt safe discussing the subject with me, it would have intensified his fears.

April 10, 1996

When Sean's cancer returned, advice began pouring in from all quarters of the population, it seemed, given out of love and concern for Sean, but given without a full understanding of the situation. Sean had no interest in alternative treatments. In fact, he was sick to death of traditional treatments as well. The doctors prescribed antibiotics to prevent a kidney infection because of the ureter stint, but Sean would not take the tablets. He was unable to swallow any medication for several months because of extreme nausea. He threw up every day and had considerable difficulty keeping food down, let alone pills. Well meaning family members sent us herbal medications with strict admonitions to use them in order to save Sean's life. We were made to feel like neglectful, almost abusive parents if we did not force those pills down his throat.

Sean tried the herbal teas relatives sent us and vomited violently. He refused to drink carrot juice or eat broccoli. One day he commented snidely, "They can drink herbal tea when they get cancer. I hope they like it better than I do." He tried some herbal medications a few months later, when his nausea was under control, but it had no effect. The unkindness of certain family members had an extremely damaging effect on me, though. For several months, there was a constant barrage of orders about what we should be doing to save Sean's life. They came in the form of accusing telephone calls, packages of the latest over the counter cancer medications in the mail, and letters describing in detail their amazement over our neglecting to seek alternative cancer treatment for Sean.

When Sean was in the hospital in December after the relapse and I was desperate with grief, someone in the family said (when I foolishly divulged that we were not pursuing alternative treatments at that time), "How can you and Al determine whether Sean lives or dies?"

How was I supposed to respond to that? The disease was determining the course of Sean's life, not our refusal to seek other forms of treatment. Some children refuse chemotherapy altogether, a decision that seems extreme to me, but how can we judge what is right for another person? There is no single answer to every problem. If I could offer one suggestion to someone who has an extended family member dying from cancer or another terminal disease, I would advise: Do not bring your own issues into the situation, and do not offer advice unless you are asked. Support is needed, not advice. The spoken word can never be taken back. Sean is gone but I am still here, and I lost the family I thought I had. I am not interested in that kind of love. That is not love, that's egotism.

I let them get to me, though, and the effects have been permanent. I still wonder if we did everything we could have for Sean. I allowed them to firmly plant that idea of neglect in my psyche, and I cannot obliterate it now.

After the relapse, I told our pediatrician I was surprised at the amount of advice flooding in. "And you will be getting a lot more," he said, nodding sympathetically. "People cannot resist it."

I especially appreciated my sister, who was quietly supportive and avoided offering advice unless I asked for it. "I do not know what to do with my own life," she said. "How can I tell someone else what to do with theirs?"

Al's mother encouraged me not to let *anyone* make me feel guilty, because I had not done anything wrong. Tyler and Al were protective as well, comparing the unkindness directed at me to someone kicking a dog who has already been hit by a car. They began intercepting phone calls, but no one seemed to direct any advice towards them; it was all reserved for me. I finally went on antidepressants because of the pressure, in order to remain cheerful for Sean.

After suffering a great deal over the judgment passed on me, I prayed about it and received a clear answer. The answer was in my head, but I could hear it as plainly as if it had been spoken out loud. "It does not matter what you do, the outcome will be the same."

I know this is a difficult concept for Westerners, because we like to think we have control over our lives, but in Sean's case, we didn't. We were not going to give up without a fight, but we refused to put him through hell. Mary shared something about my grandmother Maude, who lost a two year old daughter from infected burns, and the story helps me come to terms with things. Her little girl, Margaret, was suffering and very ill, but my grandma couldn't bear to lose her. She prayed, most fervently, that God would let her child live—at least a few more days. Little Margaret did indeed live several days before dying, and suffered greatly during that time. After witnessing such horrific anguish, my grandmother wished she had never prayed for such a thing.

I am haunted, and moved at the same time, by the story of an American couple who took their dying child to a remote location in Europe to visit the temple of a particular saint they hoped might grant their wish to save their child's life. Chemotherapy had already failed, and there was nothing left to try. The child's parents had to wheel their son in a wooden cart up a mountainside to reach the temple, where they prayed that the saint would, by some miracle, save him. Despite their monumental effort, the child died anyway. It is a heartbreaking and touching story, and I cry when I think of their desperation, but I also know that Sean would not have wanted to spend his last days being dragged across Europe and up a mountain to pray to a fickle saint. It reaffirms to me that we may not be able to do anything to prevent our death, or even to delay it. Do we really have any control over that final act in our existence here on earth?

April 18, 1996

Sean's fifteenth birthday is tomorrow. Al has a professional workshop in Idaho Falls and we are leaving tonight. We do not want to be here on his birthday. The house will be empty and remind us of our loss.

Holly, Sean's friend and English teacher, had another spiritual experience last fall, in addition to the one she had the night Sean died. I must record it before I forget, because it is reassuring when others have experiences similar to my own. It almost verifies I am not a total nut case.

The two of us had made a pact to share anything related to Sean: dreams, feelings, and so on. Holly had the first experience. She had just returned from Washington, D.C., where she was honored as Idaho's new teacher of the year. I know Sean was proud of her, but she was still grieving over him and she had decided to try prayer in order to resolve some of the overwhelming pain. Holly maintains that she does not really believe in that kind of thing, but she decided to give it a shot. She tried praying to God but ended up talking to Sean.

Suddenly, she felt his presence, so strongly that she could not deny he was in the room. Sean comforted her by communicating that he was okay and she would be too. A couple of weeks later, Holly met someone with whom she fell deeply in love. She firmly believes Sean knew it was going to happen. Is that so hard to accept, that we have spirits looking out for us and Sean has become our guardian?

April 24, 1996

I want another concrete experience. Call it greed, but I am not willing to give Sean up. It is not difficult for me to imagine another world out there, a world we cannot see with our myopic eyes. For purely cerebral and literal minds, it must be nearly impossible to believe in life after death and the notion of God and angels. But I don't think anyone will be punished for disbelief, even if it is all true in the end. You can only believe what you are able to, and for me, my beliefs are a gift. I caution myself not to use them to judge others who are unable to open themselves up to the possibility of another reality.

I want to be with Sean again, and last month I could not even dream about him. If I could wish on a dream, I would. It just doesn't work that way. I have been so desperate for him that I lost some weight during the month of March, but I have gained it all back. Being thin is one of those things I am not going to get in life, and it's all right. All the little stuff has faded into the distance, classified as useless and unworthy of using up my time and energy. Physical attractiveness is near the top of the "little stuff." If people spent more time developing their minds rather than their bodies, the world would be much better off.

SEAN

I miss Sean every day. He is a lot like his dad, which is one reason I feel the loss so deeply. We have noticed something almost eerie: Hayley is resembling Sean in appearance and behavior. Other people notice it too. She often has one of Sean's facial expressions, and Al and I glance at each other with comforting recognition. Hayley has Sean's hair and skin color, teeth, body frame (except for my round behind, lucky her), big feet, and mouth. She also has Sean's sensitivity. The similarity, in both appearance and mannerisms, is uncanny. Hayley even makes a supreme and repeated effort to hug and kiss us every night before bedtime, as Sean did long before he got sick. No matter how late it was, he always came downstairs for a good night kiss and a hug, as if he knew he had limited time to show us his love. Sometimes it alarms me that Hayley is insistent on doing the same.

Sean's birthday was last Friday. Al and I thought about him all day, though we were in Idaho Falls, which helped a bit. I hoped Sean would magically appear or contact us on the telephone, but nothing happened. On Sunday night, however, I finally dreamed about him for the first time in weeks. It was not a terribly significant dream. We were just hanging out and enjoying each other's company, but I felt wonderful when I woke up. Later that day, though, a heavy melancholy set in. Initially, the comforting experience makes you feel good, but then the reality wipes away the solace. Even if your lost child is all right, you cannot be with him, and that is the real hurt. You can't see him, or hug and kiss him good night, and the fact that you have to remain on earth is sometimes unbearable. But this time there is an interesting footnote.

When I took Hayley to school on Monday morning, she asked me if I had dreamed about Sean the night before. Hayley has had two or three meaningful dreams about her brother, and she always talks about them in hushed tones, as if they are mysterious secrets. In one dream, Sean said he loved her. In another, he held out his hand to give her a high five.

"How did you know I dreamed about Sean?" I asked.

"Because I did too," Hayley answered with a sly smile. In her dream, she was walking off the playground at Sawtooth, the elementary school she and her brothers attended. She spotted Sean with a couple of friends, kids she had never seen before. They were playing a game, clapping hands and laughing. Hayley knew they were dead, but she was the only one who could see them. None of her own friends could see Sean playing with his spirit buddies.

I believe it was meaningful. Maybe Sean was letting Hayley know he was with her too, and this might be his way of telling us he is having some fun in heaven. I entertain visions of a studious Sean, learning about astronomy, mathematics, music, the history of the universe, etc. He has a brilliant mind and academics were easy for him. I assume he spends all his time learning the wonderful secrets we are denied on earth, but perhaps I have missed something. Maybe Sean is spending some time being a kid too. When I dream about him, he is always happy, and when he appeared to me several weeks ago he had a huge grin on his face. Sean does something else while he is away from us, living in that other dimension. He spends a lot of time offering comfort. But there is more to this story.

Kelly, Sean's teacher friend, sent us a cookie basket and card on his birthday. He had been on her mind for several days in a row, especially on his birthday. She has been very involved in helping kids at the junior high raise money for Sean's memorial, and was asked to speak to a class of 7th graders who did not know Sean. They had been complaining about having to raise money for someone they didn't even know. At first, Kelly was angry at their indifference, but she quickly channeled it to help them understand how important Sean was to those who knew and loved him.

Kelly also took her homeroom class to the cemetery one day, and they cleaned the grounds, picked up trash, and so on. On another occasion her students were complaining about all the reading they had to do in her class, and she delivered an impassioned speech about being thankful for what you have. Kelly explained how much Sean loved to read, and that for the last few weeks of his life he could not, because tumors were pressing on the optic nerve and his vision was blurry and double. He had to wear an eye patch, and even that was not enough to allow him to focus. Her students (who all knew Sean) grew quiet, but the message was appropriately conveyed. Try to be grateful for what you have, because tomorrow it may be gone.

Kelly telephoned Monday evening and shared that she'd had a dream about Sean on Sunday night, as Hayley and I did. She had never dreamed about him before. In Kelly's dream, Sean was in a classroom at O'Leary. Casey and some other kids were there, and Sean was at the front of the room lying on a hospital bed. Kelly is still haunted by memories of the pain Sean suffered before he died, but in the dream he got out of bed and walked towards her. He was perfectly fine, free of the back pain and gnawing ache in his head and arms, and he began teasing her, just like old times. She was elated to see him smiling and back to normal.

Oddly, Sean was in a particular teacher's room who had taught in Montana, where Kelly attended school as a young girl. This teacher was in the classroom with Sean, and Kelly recalled that he had died of cancer a few years ago. Sean did not know him on this earth. Does he know him now?

We all dreamed about Sean on the *same* night, after weeks of not dreaming about him. It was not a coincidence. It was a gift from Sean.

April 27, 1996

Mary telephoned the other night, after listening to a television show about psychics. It happened to be on in the background while she was working in the kitchen, but she wasn't paying much attention until one of the participants complained about having trouble with his telephone after someone close to him had died. The psychic confirmed that interfering with the telephone lines is one of the most common avenues the dead use to contact the living. Mary listened more carefully, because she knew about our experiences. If spirits have altered electromagnetic fields after coming in contact with the light of God, they could easily tamper with electrical lines.

Why not?

Something else intrigues me. I was watching the film *A Passage to India* the other day. I read the E.M. Forster book years ago and had seen the film, but I could not quote a single line verbatim. About a year ago, when I was deciding what to do about Sean's course of treatment after the relapse, I was debating whether we should try some other things besides chemotherapy and radiation. But what? I was tortured by guilt and uncertainty, when I suddenly heard a clear voice. *"It does not matter what you do, the outcome will be the same."*

I quoted this in a previous entry, and I know that

westerners could offer a hundred different arguments refuting that statement, but in our case, I think it was true. One has to exercise tremendous courage to do what one believes is right, especially in the face of criticism from others. But that is not the only voice I heard during Sean's illness. A few months after his relapse, when I wondered if he was going to suffer indefinitely and if the agony would stretch on for years, the following message was relayed: *"It won't be much longer now."*

At that time, I was skeptical about guardian angels and did not fully trust the spiritual messages I had received, but in retrospect it all seems clear. Sean died shortly after those words were communicated.

I finally understand, a year later, that all the voices and premonitions were correct. Everything communicated to me, everything I thought I was imagining, was the truth. I hadn't had a meaningful dream before Sean got sick, not in 35 years of living, and I certainly had not heard any spiritual communications. I am not a mystic, but I know what I have seen and I know what I've heard. If they are gifts from Sean, or from a spiritual source in another dimension, it would be shortsighted for me to ignore them.

I was feeling particularly hopeless the other day, before I watched the film *A Passage to India*. In one section of the movie, a Hindu philosophy professor informs an English colleague that the situation regarding a mutual friend, Dr. Aziz, is already decided. This annoys his English friend, since Westerners like to think they can influence how things turn out. And I suppose they can, if it happens to work out that way. Some things, however, are already decided, but we do not know this, which leads us to theories about karma and destiny. Most Americans disregard the possibility, because they think it encourages complacency and inaction, but it doesn't have to. I will continue trying to change what I think I can, rather than letting myself be acted upon, but I am learning to accept more than I used to. Perhaps the time of our birth and death is predestined, even if nothing else is.

Stephen Hawking sums it up in one of his essays about Black Holes and Baby Universes:

"One cannot base one's conduct on the idea
that everything is determined....Instead, one
has to adopt the effective theory that one
has free will and that one is responsible
for one's actions. Is everything determined?
The answer is yes, it is. But it might as well
not be, because we can never know what is
determined."

In *A Passage To India*, the Englishman asks the Hindu professor if he likes their mutual friend; he's puzzled over the apparent indifference to the fate of Dr. Aziz. The Hindu answers matter–of–factly, "It is of no consequence if I care or do not care. The outcome is already decided." The Englishman argues that they have a responsibility to do all they can for Aziz (which I agree with), but the professor holds fast to his beliefs.

The frustrated Englishman cries, "Do nothing? Is that your philosophy?"

The Hindu calmly repeats himself. "My philosophy is, do what you like, but it will not change the outcome."

Those words hit me like a bolt of lightening. I sat up straight and listened to them again and again. I had heard the same words a year ago when I was debating whether to convince Sean to try alternative medicine. A firm voice communicated that it did not matter what we chose to do; it would not change the outcome, not in this case. I began wondering if I had dreamed up that communication from memories of seeing that film in the past, but I know I did not. I couldn't quote a single line from *A Passage To India*, and I had not seen or read it for several years.

Perhaps one of my friends on the other side was a Hindu on earth. What he or she advised was true as far as Sean was concerned, and I knew this deep in my heart. The passage of time had to verify it, though. For someone raised as an American and traditional Christian, this is a mind–boggling theory. Does this mean that Hindu beliefs are part of the whole that comprises eternal truth? Without a doubt. I have always believed religion is the response of people who are trying to explain the world in which they live. All religions contain certain truths which will travel with us to the next life. The concept of destiny and karma may be one of them.

April 28, 1996

My father has been dead for a few years, but I dreamed about him last night. In the dream, I was wandering aimlessly, crying and feeling lonely and abandoned. "I want my dad, I want my dad," I repeated several times. Suddenly, he materialized and his face was somber. He put his arms around me, and we hugged each other. I actually felt his embrace.

It seemed very real.

When we are in desperate need, I think our deceased loved ones may visit us in our dreams to offer comfort and empathy. To ignore their gift and pass it off as coincidence or self–invention is like throwing it back in their face. We need to learn to accept these spiritual offerings as demonstrations of support and love.

"Sean was here—"

MAY

SEAN

I know that I am.
I know that another is who knows more than I,
who takes an interest in me, whose creature,
and yet whose kindred in one sense, am I.
I know that the enterprise is worthy.
I know that things work well.
I have heard no bad news.

—Henry David Thoreau

May 1, 1996

A few weeks before Sean died he began expressing appreciation for what I did for him. "I know why you're so tired," he would say. "Because you wait on me all day." Or, "You're the best mom. I am really lucky."

I wasn't the best mom and Sean was not all that lucky, but he was trying to say goodbye, sharing what was in his heart. He was a quiet boy and left much unsaid, but not the important things. We knew he loved us, but I wonder if he knew how much we loved him. The last weeks of his life, my love for Sean overshadowed all else. He was literally everything to me, and I was terrified of losing him.

I asked him if he wanted to try something new, relating to his treatment. "I'll do anything you want me to, Mom," he replied. "Anything at all."

I responded with a statement that seems cruel to me now. "Just live, Sean," I said desperately. "Please—just live."

He didn't answer. How could he? I feel terrible about saying that now, as if it were in his power to grant my impossible request.

Al and I thought we could deal with Sean's death occurring at some undetermined point in the future, because we were continually surprised he was still alive, and as long as he was alive we could be cheerful because we still had our boy. Every day was a gift. As long as

Sean was laughing and joking, it was bearable. But he finally quit laughing and found it impossible to enjoy what he used to. That final month, he was unable to watch television because it was difficult for him to concentrate and see. The growing tumors were pressing on the optic nerve, and his vision was rapidly deteriorating. The bone pain was widespread. Sean's left arm was almost useless, the numbness in his chin ever present, and the growths on the back of his head had converged into a single, giant, bumpy mass. A new tumor in the middle of his chest, at the sternum, appeared suddenly. I could only imagine what was happening inside his tortured body.

Terror gripped my failing spirits when I approached Sean about the new tumor. "Sean, when did this appear? How long has it been there?"

He shook his head and said tiredly, "I don't know." I noticed a beaten look, a wave of defeat spreading across Sean's pale face.

I was in close contact with the doctors in Salt Lake during the month of July, and I even asked about treating Sean with the big time chemos again. They did not recommend it; he was obviously resistant to the extensive chemotherapy he had already had. Repeating the process would make him sicker and increase the danger of Sean dying in the hospital. We wanted to avoid a depressing hospitalization. Sean needed to be at home.

A few months before, in January, he had to be hospitalized locally for what we thought was an infection. When cancer patients run high fevers while their white counts are low, it is standard procedure to hospitalize them so that intravenous antibiotics can be administered. The final evening of that particular hospitalization, the doctor announced that Sean could go home. Al and I were attending Tyler's basketball game that night, so it was more convenient for us to leave Sean there until morning. We arranged to take Sean home in the morning, and his physician returned to the nurses' desk to write the orders.

After the doctor left the room, Sean started crying. He tried to mask his emotions by biting his lip, but huge tears streamed down his hollow cheeks. He was unable to speak, but I understood what he was trying to say. He could not stand being there one more hour; another night seemed like cruel and unusual punishment. I walked out to the nurses' desk and tearfully told the doctor that I wanted to take Sean home immediately.

I cannot believe I was so selfish. Having cancer was not convenient, especially for Sean, and if he was well enough to be at home, it was up to us to make it happen. From then on I tried to arrange hospital discharges at the earliest possible date. I hounded doctors, and we kept Sean at home as much as we could. He did not deserve to suffer any more than he had to. Sean was saturated by medical treatments.

He'd had it.

May 2, 1996

By July of 1995, I had accepted that the end was here, but the reality sometimes sent me into a full–blown panic attack. Sean couldn't die. I could not live if he was dead. A few days before his death, I shared my deepest feelings.

"I don't know how I can go on without you, Sean. You are my closest friend and dearest confidante."

"Well," he answered matter–of–factly and rather coldly, "you'll have to, because I'm not going to be around."

The morphine he was medicated with throughout July was a mixed blessing, even when we switched to the pump, which dripped the strongest form of pain medication into his battered system. It failed to take care of all the pain. His right arm continually ached and the head pain became intense. He was developing a tolerance to all medication, and he had uncontrollable tremors in response to the morphine.

We tried patches and other kinds of pain medication, but they did not work as well as the morphine. One particular day, Sean was suffering from horrifying head pain just before we switched to the IV pump. I gave him 90 milligrams of oral morphine and injected a shot of morphine into his thigh as well. I was worried that I had overdosed him, but instead, it had no effect. Sean lay on my bed, crying, holding his head for three hours until the pain subsided. If I had it to do over again, I would have put him on the morphine pump sooner, but even that was not enough. It didn't fix everything.

He was able to talk about dying the last week or so. Kidney failure was imminent, and he was putting out very little urine. His abdomen, especially around his right kidney, was visibly swollen. "What is *this*?" he cried as he stared at his abdomen. I explained why the kidney was distended and encouraged him to distract himself. But he couldn't, and it was a stupid and naive suggestion on my part. No distraction could disguise the betrayal of his own body.

Sean had read the book *Embraced by the Light,* an account of one woman's detailed near death experience, and he found comfort and truth in the book. We discussed life after death and I think he believed in it, but my own theories are firmer now. I wish I had prepared him more. If I knew then what I know now, I could have done a better job in helping our boy face his uncertain future. I was sadly inept, though Sean did not appear to be as afraid of what would happen after death as he was over the process.

"Will it hurt?" he asked fearfully. "How will I actually die?"

None of us knew what to expect. I assured him it would not be painful, but for all I knew that might have been a lie.

A week before Sean died, I took Hayley away from the house and told her that her brother was definitely going to die. The possibility had been discussed before, but neither Tyler nor Hayley believed it would actually happen. I explained that Sean was going to leave us and live with God. I pretended that I knew what was going to happen to him, that he would be fine and that we would see him again some day, but it was all guesswork. I didn't *know* whether he would be all right or not. I didn't *know* if I would see him again.

Hayley's big hazel eyes filled with tears, and she pulled her hand back and hit me hard on my upper arm. I tried to hug her, but she would not allow me to. I imagine she was thinking, "How can Mom tell such an awful lie about Sean?"

We are going to Washington in a couple of days to accept the Spirit of Community award for Sean. I do not want to go anymore; it is going to be very difficult. We feel propelled by something beyond ourselves, though. Perhaps it is Sean. I read a poem by Edgar Allan Poe that might apply here:

> "The spirits of the dead who stood in life
> before thee, are again in death around thee
> and their will shall overshadow thee: be still."

SEAN

All right, Sean. I'll be still. I will try to listen, and especially, to believe.

May 10, 1996

We survived the trip to Washington and the award ceremonies. It was tough, but we were amazingly calm. After we arrived at our hotel, though, Hayley came down with the flu. She was staying overnight with Kelly, and afterwards Al's mom, and when I talked to her on the telephone the second night we were there, she cried. I wanted to go home immediately. It was reminiscent of Sean. I could not be away from him when he was sick. But I convinced myself it was only the flu and we didn't go home. I refuse to leave Hayley again, though, not until she is older. The time we have with our children passes too soon.

Suddenly, it is over.

We met some incredible kids and their parents in Washington who were touched by Sean's story. It is not an original story, I know, but they were interested. We had to talk about Sean a lot more than I was comfortable with, but there was a definite spirit in this group of 104 young people who were being honored for volunteer work. We were motivated by their selflessness. In addition to the $1,000 memorial award, Sean received one of fifteen national awards, and I gave a short speech at the National Press Club about not giving up. During the final weeks of Sean's life, after the tumors on his head were verified as metastasis, I offered him an alternative. He didn't have to continue treatment. We would support whatever decision he made.

I don't know how I expected Sean to respond, but he certainly was not grateful for my suggestion. He looked at me like I was crazy and said, "But that would be giving up, Mom. I am *not* giving up."

I have shared that story a few times, but it's a timeless message. Cherish life until it is taken from you. No matter how hopeless your life seems, or the world seems, never give up. Sean had a lot more courage than I have, though. I have come dangerously close to giving up.

The day we left for home, one of the honorees' mothers walked up to me and said, "Continue to tell your son's story. It's very important, you know."

I was a little surprised by her comment, especially since Sean's story has probably reached an end, or it will after the dedication to the memorial at the end of this month. I don't think I will have any more opportunities to speak about him in public. I am planning to return to my private shell.

Visiting the Holocaust Museum in Washington was a poignant, horrifying experience, but it could not be missed. I felt a continual presence beside me throughout the museum visit, and though I am sensitive to Sean's spirit now, I was not sure it was him. Why would he follow me around in the Holocaust museum? Perhaps the presence was a Holocaust survivor, I finally decided, though that didn't make much sense since I am not Jewish.

We listened to the testimonials of survivors, and I was especially touched by the comments of Gerda Weismann Klein, who wrote *All But My Life,* an account of the time she spent in Nazi concentration camps. She talked about the survivors and how they had to develop the attitude of never giving up, no matter how bad it got. Her remarks mirrored Sean's, in response to a different, crueler source of pain and suffering.

After we left the museum four hours later, the spiritual presence remained strong for a couple of hours. Now I believe it was Sean, because he stayed with me for so long. I wonder why he chose that particular time, though.

May 25, 1996

The memorial service at O'Leary Junior High is over. I was dreading it because I was the main speaker, but I felt compelled to share my thoughts about Sean. Who knew him better than I? Holly and Casey spoke as well, along with Wiley Dobbs, the principal. Wiley shared what it was like when he started chemotherapy for Hodgkins disease a few months after Sean was diagnosed. "Oh, Mr. Dobbs," Sean had reassured, "chemotherapy is not that bad."

"Actually, Sean lied about that," he offered with a smile.

Hailey Hodges read the inscription on the bronze plaque, and Casey talked about his friendship with Sean. Congressman Crapo's aide presented an honorarium check for $1,000 to the memorial fund, in memory of Sean. That last generosity brought us up to our goal. There is enough to pay for the entire project. The O'Leary students gave up pizza parties, sold cans of soda and bottles of water, and brought in their own cash to raise money for the memorial. When Hailey Hodges ran for student body president the previous fall, she had promised to make sure Sean Miller was remembered. She won the election. I am so proud of their selflessness.

The memorial service went well. It was held outside around the landscaped memorial, but only the 9th graders attended because the school facilities are too small to accommodate all 900 students. We flew Tyler home from the Academy for the service, which in some ways was more enlightening than the funeral—probably because those who loved Sean the most were able to talk about him publicly.

I have an intense fear of getting up in front of people, and I was afraid I could not pull this one off without some help from Sean. Al and I had a rare disagreement a couple of days before and I was really angry at him. I can't remember being that angry, not for a long time. I was full of bitter feelings, and I didn't know how I could speak to those students and motivate them when I was full of darkness myself. It was too late to cancel, but if there had been any way to do it, I would have. Holly telephoned a couple of hours before the service, and I wept when I heard her sympathetic voice. She was calm and reassured me that everything would be okay, but I wasn't sure. There was only one alternative. I needed God, or Sean, to help me pull this one off. I attempted to pray, and asked for help to step out of the anger.

What followed was a blessing. The feelings of bitterness were swept away and replaced by a peaceful calm. I had a miraculous change of heart. By the time I got up to speak, I wasn't nervous and was able to convey the message that I felt was important. I was so grateful for the help, from whoever was responsible. If I hadn't had a change of attitude, I could not have talked about Sean in the way he deserved. It was nothing short of a miracle.

Holly has been going through some rough times. She is living in Ketchum now and believes the major reason she came to Twin Falls to teach was to meet Sean and become his friend. She gave an excellent talk at the memorial service and called Sean an *old soul*, partly because he seemed to know things the rest of us didn't. He also didn't need to run off at the mouth. He said things once, and if you were not listening, you missed it. Holly cautioned the students to use their time wisely and not give up their time on earth by becoming involved in the party scene. She pointed out that Sean's education was of prime importance to him. He used his time carefully, and he had very little of it to work with. Then she dropped a bombshell.

Holly was diagnosed with cervical cancer a few weeks ago (at 26 years old), but she is all right now, after a successful surgery. It is the kind of cancer that can recur, though, and it will always be in the background, waving a warning flag across her future. This gives her relationship with Sean even greater significance and strengthens the spiritual connection. But I was shocked and saddened by her news. Was it coincidence that Sean and Holly met and became friends? I don't think so. Perhaps coincidence does not exist.

Wiley presented Hayley, Tyler, Al, and me with the 1995–96 school yearbook, which is dedicated to Sean. It is a kind and loving page long tribute, and I cannot thank them enough.

The service concluded with an a cappella song performed by a boys quartet from the high school, "*Prayer of the Children.*" It was beautiful.

The fanfare is over and I am overwhelmingly grateful for what has been done, but I want to return to my reclusiveness and private grief. I won't be talking about Sean in public anymore.

May 28, 1996

When Sean was a baby, I used to race home from school to spend an hour alone with him before I picked Tyler up from day care. Rocking and kissing my babies was one of the best parts of motherhood, but one particular occasion stands out. I was home early that afternoon, and six-month-old Sean and I were alone in the apartment. I rocked and held him, and remember feeling that this child was incredibly special.

Sean was not as even featured as his two siblings, and as an infant, he was fat and had brown hair that stuck up all over his round head like he was electrified. When Tyler and Hayley were little, people stopped us all the time and commented on their pretty faces. I don't remember anyone doing that with Sean, though he was certainly cute enough to have merited the occasional remark. I can only imagine how parents of handicapped children must feel, never being told they have a darling child, facing pity in people's eyes instead of admiration. If only the rest of us could see what a child's parent sees.

Indeed, I saw something different in Sean that day. When I looked into his small brown eyes nearly sixteen years ago, I saw a strangely mature human being, as if his spirit was revealing itself, trying to tell me something before it forgot. Sean's soul communicated with me, though he had the body of an infant. I knew things would be different with him.

I just didn't know how.

SEAN

JUNE

SEAN

And which of us,
seeing that nothing is outside
the vast wide-meshed net of heaven,
knows just how it is cast?

The Way of Life
—Lao Tzu

June 2, 1996

Memorial Day was kind of nice. My mother sent money for an arrangement for Sean's grave, and I ordered a combination of white and blue tipped carnations with wild greens and a blue ribbon with gold lettering that read, "*We Love Sean.*" Several of Sean's friends left flowers and notes on his grave, on a much larger scale than they had done at Christmas. At the memorial service I had emphasized that the little things really make a difference, and his classmates followed through by covering Sean's grave with memorial tributes.

Whenever we see his old friends, they always say "Hello," and ask how we're doing. Instead of running away because they are uncomfortable and afraid of what to say, they meet us with concern and a smile. I will never forget the people who were kind to Sean, like a couple of his elementary teachers who kept in touch during his illness and sent gifts and letters. It would have been easier for them to distance themselves from the pain.

One of my favorite photos came from one of Sean's baseball buddies, who came to the house the day after Sean died. He was with his parents and older brother, and they were all crying, especially the boys. They gave us a framed 8 x 10 photograph of a smiling Sean and four baseball friends with their arms around each other, taken at a tournament the summer before he was diagnosed with cancer.

It is a remembrance of happier, carefree days.

SEAN

June 6, 1996

I am nostalgic, and not just for our family of five. I feel a constant nostalgia for earlier years, particularly the 1800's and early 1900's. Whenever I reread *A Child's Christmas in Wales,* by Dylan Thomas, I am deeply touched with a mixture of joy and longing for a time and place I have never lived in. I also have the video, with the classic actor Denholm Elliot, and when the weather gets cold and blustery, I slip it into the VCR and watch it, though Christmas may be months away. It satisfies a deep longing for something we are missing now, something I have never experienced. I grew up during the rock 'n roll, Vietnam era; nothing was innocent and beautiful.

I have my share of good memories from my childhood, but I have the other kind too. When I was 7 years old, we lived in a trailer in a Nevada casino town. My mother had to go to work, and my gentle father's alcoholism was worsening. I was unaware he had a drinking problem until I discovered an enormous cache of empty whiskey bottles stashed beneath the trailer.

My charming, loving father was an alcoholic.

I was deeply saddened, and horrified as well, but those were the days of keeping family secrets, so I kept it to myself. Our parents loved us deeply and we loved them, but the five children (I was the youngest) were wounded by the continual chaos in our lives.

After my discovery, I understood a lot of mysteries in my past, like the vague memory of the police coming to my grandmother's door when I was five years old. They were asking about my dad, and as I hid behind my grandma, I heard her say, "Oh no, he wouldn't have done that. Not my son." I still do not know what my father was accused of, but it was probably related to his drinking. My discovery of his alcoholism also explained the fighting at home and the resentment my parents had for each other. They were overwhelmed with everything they had to deal with: a house full of children, a lack of education and money, and the dreaded alcoholism driving a wedge between them. It must have been so difficult.

As I grew older, I remember thinking that the best thing you can give a child is parents who love each other. I desperately wanted my parents to love each other, but they did not. The love, perhaps, was hidden beneath all the pain. Now I see things a bit differently. The best gift my parents gave me was *their* love. I knew I was loved, and that is what a child needs most. Parents who love each other are a bonus.

Besides, maybe they were more in love than they realized. When my mother became pregnant with me, she was 39 and my father was 46. They had no money, four older children were living at home, and my mom was caring for her dying mother. In those circumstances, news of another mouth to feed was hardly welcome. But when my mother told my dad she was pregnant again, he smiled and said encouragingly, "Well, I can stand it if you can."

Despite their often insurmountable problems, they were facing the cold world together, and the reason my maternal grandmother was living with them during her last days was because my dad had encouraged it. He was kind to my grandmother, and that had to mean a lot to my mom.

I am thankful my childhood was less than perfect. How could I have coped with adulthood if everything had gone my way? I am now glad that I was not protected, because seeing the sordid side of life convinced me I didn't want that. I saw nothing interesting or intriguing about ugliness. It held no fascination for me.

I want to see and read something inspiring. Perhaps

the grace and simplicity of earlier days only exists in literature and film, but I still want it. I need some thread of hope that the depravity in the world is not obliterating all the beauty. I have particular disdain for cop movies in general; I don't want to hear the word *fuck* reiterated in every other sentence like it's a cultural motif. Vulgarity no longer seems interesting, and it certainly isn't shocking.

Bad language used to escape my attention, I admit, and we have always taken our kids to all sorts of movies because we did not believe in using babysitters at night. We wanted our children to be with us whenever possible, but now I am confronted with the absolute lack of humanity and beauty in a society whose young people get their sense of culture from MTV and VH–1. Some of us are wandering around in a state of mass confusion, occasionally getting a handle on things, but most of the time just floating.

I want to escape to another world, but I am stuck in this one. It can be so disappointing.

June 15, 1996

I was at the bookstore the other day, and I saw a teacher I used to work with who lost her husband to cancer a couple of years ago. She's had a lot to deal with, including a son with cerebral palsy. When her husband was originally diagnosed, the cancer was successfully treated. He had been in remission for five years when it returned. He went through chemo and radiation again, but the cancer moved rapidly into his liver and brain, and he died the following year, after several strokes and much suffering.

"If you had it to do over again with Sean," she asked, "would you do anything differently?"

The old feelings of not having done everything we should have for Sean returned, and I felt my heart sink. "Well," I answered with hesitation, "what we did for him did not work. But I don't think we could have done anything else." I didn't want to get into all the guilt and recriminations. I had been through that too many times.

"What about you?" I asked tentatively, trying to be polite. I did not really want to know what she had to say. I was afraid she would plunge into a discussion of alternative medicine and share her regrets over having chosen traditional treatment instead of herbs, vitamins, and dietary therapy to cure her husband's cancer. I didn't want to hear it. Hindsight could not help me now.

But her response was the direct opposite of what I expected. "If we had to do it again," she replied thoughtfully, "we would have done nothing. The second time around my husband didn't respond to treatment, and although additional chemo and radiation bought more time, it was not *good* time. He was extremely ill. I should have let him go."

You cannot imagine how much that helped me. It was better than any therapy session.

June 20, 1996

Sean seems so far gone. How can he be gone? Where did he go? Today I saw a little boy at the grocery store with cancer. He was five or six and walking around with his sister and two younger siblings. His broviac tubes were hanging out of his T–shirt, and he was pale and bald. My heart leaped with recognition, like I was seeing Sean again. I wanted to run after the child and hug him, but the cashier was having problems with the register and I was stuck in line. I caught sight of him a few moments later, but then he disappeared.

I struggled with my emotions all the way to the car and cried on the drive home. I kept saying out loud, "Bless his heart. Bless his sweet little heart." Most people don't know what that child has endured, but Sean knows, because he was there. I had a similar experience a few months ago, when I was shopping and saw a nine or ten year old boy with tumors on the back of his head, similar to Sean's, but smaller. I sank into depression. I cannot see a young boy with a bald head anymore without crying.

My concept of beauty is different now. Children with cancer are beautiful, far more engaging than kids with thick hair and rosy cheeks. There is something unearthly about them, something precious and fragile.

I want my cancer child back.

June 25, 1996

House Beautiful magazine called today, and they want to publish an article I sent them. I am so excited! You would think I had just sold my first novel for half a million dollars. It's an essay about Sean and our house that I submitted only two weeks ago, so I was surprised to hear from them. I am used to getting most of my manuscripts back with a form letter rejection enclosed.

They are publishing it in the Christmas issue.

A few weeks ago I decided that Sean's story had come to an end, at least publicly, but the idea for the essay suddenly popped into my head and I felt compelled to write it. This is a miracle, selling my first piece to a major magazine. I have to keep writing and let things flow. Admittedly, most of my efforts are abortive, but that is all right for now. Someday things may be different.

I have chosen to do something that is bound to send me alternately into despair and exhilaration, a poor combination for someone who is battling depression, but I can't back out now. Sean always encouraged me to write. A few months before his death, he said, "It's going to happen, Mom. It is just a matter of when." When I first started writing seriously, I received a lot of rejections and I was not used to the emotional battering. One day I was feeling particularly desperate, but my boys brought me down to earth.

"If I can handle not making the varsity basketball team this year," Tyler argued, "you can handle a simple rejection."

"Yeah, Mom," Sean piped in, "if I can handle having cancer, you can handle this."

I suddenly felt ridiculous, but I am glad they had the courage to tell me what they thought. Neither of them wasted any time feeling sorry for themselves. Why should I?

A couple of months ago, we decided that I was not going back to teaching this year. I feel, for no logical reason, that this is the right thing to do, and Al supports me as he always has. But abandoning logic is not easy, because following your heart can sometimes backfire.

We all need to be less afraid of making mistakes, however. What we have on earth is time, and maybe we don't need to be in such a hurry to accomplish certain goals by a pre–determined date. We will never arrive at the finish line. We have an eternity ahead of us. What to do next, though, is a serious issue. I need some kind of focus.

June 30, 1996

The one advantage of having a really bad day is that the next one is always better. When I spend an entire day plunged into abject misery, I wake up the next morning and invariably think, "At least it's not yesterday!" I appreciate the good days now.

I also realize that I am hanging on by a thread, and that what I think today may be somewhat different tomorrow. I am more dependent on a spiritual force to love and guide me, and perhaps I need to feel that way. A friend of mine calls me a *free lance believer*. I love that.

I am a solitary person, though, and I like to think that everything I have accomplished, I have done by myself. But now I wonder if there are unseen hands guiding me. I do not believe God expects us to trudge through this life alone. I think He and His angels are helping us, and we have to learn to communicate with them. I stopped trying for years, but I cannot live like that anymore. When I gave up religion, I thought I had to give up God.

What a misconception.

"Sean was here—"

JULY

SEAN

Who are you my child and darling?
Who are you sweet boy
with cheeks yet blooming?

"A Sight in Camp in the Daybreak Gray and Dim"
—Walt Whitman

July 7, 1996

We spent the first weekend at the cabin as a family. Al started building it last summer when Sean was still alive. The tumors in his head hadn't appeared when we made plans to have the logs delivered, and we had no reason to assume he would not have another remission. He had a tremendous response to chemotherapy the first time around. Why couldn't it happen again? But it failed to turn out the way we planned, and the cabin was finished too late for Sean to enjoy.

I was not sure I would want to spend any time there because Sean couldn't, and building that place had been a source of a few disagreements between Al and me. Privately I vowed to hate it, but I am afraid I will not be able to keep my promise. It is casting a spell on me with its peace and remote location. There is no electricity, no television or phone. Those details alone are enough to make me like the place.

I don't care about the things I do when I am running the middle class wheel in the flatlands, like being clean or having an agenda, and Hayley and Al are in love with the land. We took several long walks last weekend and floated the river. Al still has a lot of finish work to do, but we had some private time too.

I worry about how we are going to afford to keep the cabin, of course, but Al thrives on challenges. It gives him a reason for working, I suppose, and it keeps him optimistic. Every weekend he heads for the hills and

213

always returns in a good mood. It used to bother me that Al had to leave home to gain some peace of mind, but I think I understand. That place in the mountains is a sanctuary. We all need somewhere to heal our wounds. This house, where Sean's memory resides within these walls, is mine, but Al needed something different.

Last year at this time, Sean was dying. The final morning of his life, on August 3rd, his breathing had become labored, and by afternoon he was struggling for every breath, as Dr. O'Brien had predicted. He was not responding to us and had slipped into a coma. He lost control of his bodily functions, and Tyler and I had to clean him up several times. Sean would have been humiliated, but I was glad to do it. I *wanted* to take care of him; I didn't want his life to end. As I watched his condition become critical, I even considering returning him to the hospital to receive the blood transfusion I had refused a week before. But it was too late for that. I was horrified that the end had finally come.

The day of his death, Sean had an ugly sore on his ankle where it had rubbed against his leg the night before. Similar sores appeared on his chin and chest. His face was grossly swollen, which distorted his appearance and frightened Hayley, Tyler, and even me. His eyes were puffy, and his right ear was twice the size of the other one because he had leaned his head towards that side during the night. Every time I looked at him, I cried.

Al got home from work mid–afternoon, finally convinced that this was the end. A few weeks before, he had said optimistically, "I wouldn't be surprised if Sean is still alive at Christmas." I stared at him, amazed. I doubted Sean would be alive the following month, and certainly not in December. But at that point, Al was unable to accept the truth.

"I can't believe this is happening!" I cried. I had plenty of time to believe it would happen, but forewarning does not make the end any easier. That's a popular misconception, that being able to say goodbye makes it easier. We never really said goodbye anyway, because Sean didn't want to talk about his impending death. I am grateful we had as long as we did, but I don't know that it was any *easier.* If anything, I learned to love and miss him even more.

Hayley was with her grandma and aunt the day Sean died, and they brought her home about 6 P.M.. They had intended going to a movie that Hayley wanted to see, but oddly, she wanted to come home instead.

Tyler sat down to watch a sitcom in the kitchen, which happened to be one of Sean's favorite television programs. I encouraged him to come upstairs and watch it next to Sean, who always hated being left alone. Al and Hayley joined us after the program, and we sat in silence for a while, watching and waiting. Al and I discussed our spiritual beliefs and what we believed would happen to Sean. For the first time, Tyler anxiously asked questions about life after death. We offered and discussed our best theories. That night, I strongly believed in the existence of God; there was an otherworldly presence in the room. We could almost touch it.

Hayley and I rubbed Sean's arms and held his hands. I didn't hug him because it always hurt his bones when we embraced, but I wish I had done it anyway. At that point he could not feel the pain, and I needed to hold him. I was still operating on instinct, though. We had not been able to hug Sean for several weeks.

Instead, we sang lullabies and talked to him, expressing our love and reassuring him that it was okay to leave us and pass to the other side. His physical suffering was extreme, almost unbearable to watch, but we didn't want to leave him. Around 10 P.M., I told Al, Tyler, and Hayley that they could go to bed and I would stay with Sean. We didn't know whether we had days, hours, or minutes left. During the previous two years, Sean and I were often alone together—waiting for treatments, waiting for scans, waiting for bad news. I was used to that, but this time no one left the room.

Everyone felt drawn to our boy.

Sean was not responding, and his breathing was becoming more and more labored. His skin was jaundiced, his lips blue, and he was literally struggling for each breath. His chest rose deeper each time; he wasn't getting the air he needed. Tyler pressed the bolus button on the morphine pump a few times, hoping Sean could not feel the distress we were witnessing. At one point I left his side and searched the house for an extra syringe of morphine. We suddenly understood why some people resorted to euthanasia. It was unnatural that Sean was still alive and suffering, as if his body was programmed to continue living while his mind was long gone. But there was no extra morphine, and we resigned ourselves to watching and waiting.

At 10:25 P.M., we gathered along the sofa and held hands, each of us touching Sean. We prayed that Sean would be released from his body, and we continued to hold his hand and tell him we loved him. There was nothing else to say. But he didn't respond to our touch and lay motionless with limp hands, his eyes rolled back in his head.

Suddenly, Sean gripped my hand.

"Oh Mom," Tyler offered, "it's just a reflex."

It wasn't, though, because seconds later Sean opened his eyes and looked at me. His eyes were unfocused, but he was trying to see.

"Sean," Al said softly, "we have been with you all

night, and we won't leave. You know that, don't you?"

A couple of sounds escaped from Sean's throat as he tried to speak, but he was unable to form any words. We will never know what he was trying to say. Sometimes that really bothers me.

Moments later, his eyes rolled back in his head and he was unresponsive once more. His breathing began to slow. Soon the breaths came further apart; he was dying. He took a deep gulp of air, followed by nothing for about fifteen seconds. Sean took his last breath, more like a gasp, really, and that was it.

It was over.

Tortured, choking sobs filled the room, but we all remained in our own space. None of us embraced the other for comfort. We wanted to be left alone, like beaten dogs licking their wounds.

I wonder if Sean was watching from above his body and if he found what he saw comforting, or perhaps strange. We cried and cried until finally, we stopped. We studied Sean's face and saw, quite clearly, that his spirit was no longer there. As my brother David said when he saw his dead wife, Christine, after her car accident, "It was like looking at the envelope without the letter inside."

Tyler spoke first. "He's gone."

July 14, 1996

I asked Al if he thinks our marriage is stronger than it was before Sean's death. He said he cannot remember what it was like before. It's as if time has stopped. But I know that Al is more sympathetic and caring now, and so am I. I weigh thirty pounds more than I did when we got married, and he never says a word about it. He still thinks I'm pretty, and though the mirror does not agree with his assessment, I am glad that love is blind. I, too, love him so much that I am willing to take whatever goes along with it, bad habits, misunderstandings and natural consequences, the whole bit. We have accepted imperfection in ourselves and in each other.

It feels good.

I read about a study that focused on infant boys and girls who were only four hours old and attempted to determine whether or not the sexes respond differently on an emotional level from the onset of life. The study discovered that the female infants responded to touch and voices immediately, while the males were less interested. Men and women are vastly dissimilar. The way in which men distance themselves emotionally may be instinctive, not purposeful. We need to be tolerant of each other's differences. Patience is required.

I was driving through Gooding (a small town that is part of what I consider the *real* Idaho) last week on the way to the cabin. The state school for the deaf and blind is there, and I was reminded of a visit our nursing class made years ago to the state institution for the severely retarded in Nampa. It struck me with great force that what we do to the severely handicapped is unconscionable. We lock them up in buildings so we do not have to look at them, and parents are forced to hide their children away because society is so cruel. We are losing a valuable opportunity to learn about love, kindness, and empathy.

When Al and I were in Salt Lake City a few weeks ago, we were walking around in the mall, and I said that I could not imagine a greater tragedy for a parent than losing a child. As we continued our stroll, we noticed a family with a severely retarded teenaged son. After they had passed by, Al offered quietly, "I think they would disagree with you."

As always, I am sobered by my lack of experience. We only know about what we have experienced, and it is difficult to fully understand another person's challenges and heartaches. I recently read that the singer Phoebe Snow cares for her brain damaged daughter at home, and that she has been doing this all the child's life. Those lessons in love will have an eternal benefit.

We are grossly unaware of how much we can learn from people with handicaps, or even from people on a lower economic or intellectual level. Can we learn from people who are academically inferior to us? Absolutely. Learning is a wide, vast plain of diversity. Delusions of superiority and egotism are mankind's major stumbling blocks.

We have to learn to see things differently. Sean did, to a far greater degree than we understood. He has a cousin, my sister's son, who is several years older and has some handicaps which have created major social difficulties for him. Kristofer has never fit into the mainstream, and being different has been a source of continual pain, causing him to withdraw from others. My sister recently shared that high school was a nightmare for her eldest son. Because Kristofer suffers in silence much of the time, they were unaware that some of his fellow high school students teased him mercilessly. One year, a particular group of boys chose Kristofer as their scapegoat and threw him up against the lockers whenever he walked by, tormenting him verbally before he was allowed to leave. On one occasion, he was locked up inside a locker for several hours before being discovered. His high school life became a nightmare, despite the fact that his younger brother tried to protect him, after he became aware of what was happening. My sister didn't learn about it until long after the fact. It's no wonder that Kristofer withdrew from people. It was much safer to disconnect.

Sean treated Kristofer with respect. They played together while growing up and always found something of mutual interest to share. Sean wasn't just being kind. He simply did not think there was anything *wrong* with Kristofer. He saw his cousin differently than others did and accepted him for what he was, without hesitation.

After the funeral, Mary shared what Kristofer had said with tears in his eyes. "Sean was my favorite cousin." He carries a copy of Sean's photo and obituary in his pocket, day in and day out. I wept when I heard that.

July 20, 1996

I telephoned a friend of ours whose adult stepson was recently diagnosed with cancer. She is a medical social worker and came to the house last year to talk about death with Sean; she helped open the lines of honest communication. Sean might have resented the directness from someone else, but he accepted it from Char, partly because she had survived her own battle with cancer twenty years ago and knew about what he was going through. After we talked about her stepson for a while, she said that she was glad I had called, because she had a story to tell.

Char was vacationing in Yellowstone Park with her mother and sister a few weeks after her stepson was diagnosed. She was climbing a hill covered with wildflowers and sat down alone to think. The past few weeks, coupled with a trying year, had been uncertain and frightening, and she was practically to the breaking point. Suddenly, she felt a presence.

Char, by nature, is the queen of fun. She loves to joke and make light of things, and that's one reason she is so well liked. This time, however, she was serious. "Your son was with me," she said. "I don't know how to explain it, but he was there."

She felt that Sean was encouraging her as well as reassuring her that she had the ability to make her life a happy one. "Sean was there, Julie," she said tearfully. "I just wanted you to know."

July 21, 1996

It is 4:00 in the morning, and I cannot sleep. This has been a rough summer. I miss Sean so much. A couple of times I have driven out to the cemetery and cried on his headstone. I don't know if anyone saw me, and I no longer care. Sean has seemed far away this summer, and I hate it. I have not dreamed about him since April. I want to see him again and feel that burning in my chest, like I felt the night he appeared at my bedside. I know it was God's way of telling me that it was really Sean, in case I ever decided to doubt it. My only comfort is that he looked blissfully happy. Why can't I be happy too?

Because it is different for those of us left behind. Last night I listened to *"Fire and Rain"* by James Taylor, the song my nephew and I performed at the funeral, and I felt completely lost. There haven't been any spiritual experiences lately. Is this Sean's way of telling me I am

SEAN

on my own? Why can't I continue to have contact with him for the rest of my life? Why does it have to end?

July 22, 1996

The first year of Sean's illness, he stayed at home most of the time. We tried to get him back in school, but his treatment was so intensive that it became difficult. He would have one week of chemotherapy with the attendant nausea and vomiting, followed by a week in which his white blood cell count was dangerously low, putting him at risk of contracting an infection, and the third week he would feel reasonably well. But the following week we would return to Salt Lake City for more treatment and the cycle would begin again. Sean was not anxious to return to school on those few good days, and I enjoyed having him at home. For a kid who had always been happy at school and content among his peers, this was a new state of affairs. I think Sean was anxious, perhaps, to catch up on lost time with me. His time at home was a gift, because I didn't spend enough time with him when he was little. I was too busy and overwhelmed by responsibilities.

The doctors told us that Sean would get bored if he was at home all the time, in between the frequent hospital visits, of course. They didn't know Sean.

"Are you bored?" I asked with concern. "Is this tedious for you, day after day of staying at home?"

"Nope," he answered matter-of-factly. "I like it here. I'm not at all bored."

It was the best decision for us at the time. The

following year, as an 8th grader, he felt a bit differently. He was eager to return to school then. I think it was a good thing, because Sean had a positive influence on his peers and teachers, and they had a positive influence on him. They helped him feel like a normal kid for a few hours each day.

July 23, 1996

Hayley was a direct gift from God. Al didn't want more than two children, and we had reached an agreement almost ten years ago about not having any more. After a lengthy discussion about the pros and cons of increasing our family size, I decided to listen to logic and go back on the birth control pill. That night, remarkably, I got pregnant. Someone knew more than we did, that we would desperately need Hayley when Sean was gone.

But she won't be around forever.

As for my own future, I have to trust my feelings. I know we are supposed to figure things out for ourselves, and when we ask for guidance, maybe it doesn't come in terms of a direct answer. Maybe it is just a feeling, and that's terrifying. How we can trust our feelings? Apparently, I am going to have to try. Logic has not served me very well.

SEAN

July 24, 1996

Today I reread Sean's poem, *"The Cancer is There"*. I interpreted it differently this time, especially the passage "The Cancer is gone. 4 months go by, and you think you won't die, then you get sick, it hits you like a brick...The Cancer is there." We had never seriously considered what the "4 months go by" referred to. The only time the cancer was gone was when Sean had the bone marrow transplant, in June of 1994. He wrote the poem in October of 1994, so 4 months had to refer to the time that had elapsed since the transplant. Sean was in remission then, and outwardly confident about his chances of cure. "You think you won't die."

But the poem predicted that he was going to get sick again, some time after *"4 months go by,"* and that eventually he would die. *"Now you are dead, alone ... in your bed. The Cancer is dead."* In November, a couple of weeks after he wrote the poem, the cancer returned. Suddenly, his words had a forceful, specific impact.

Sean knew he was going to die. Despite his optimism, probably displayed for our benefit because he couldn't stand it when we were sad, he had predicted it.

But we did not understand. Perhaps we didn't want to.

AUGUST

SEAN

For what is it to die but to stand naked
in the wind and to melt into the sun?
And what is it to cease breathing,
but to free the breath from its restless tides,
that it may rise and expand
and seek God unencumbered?

Only when you drink from the river of
silence shall you indeed sing.
And when you have reached the mountaintop,
then you shall begin to climb.
And when the earth shall claim your limbs,
then shall you truly dance.

"On Death"

—Kahlil Gibran, *The Prophet*

August 3, 1996

Today is the anniversary of Sean's death. It has been, undoubtedly, the worst year of my life, and I am not sure the next year will be any better. But I cannot predict the future. How do I know it will be endlessly sad? How do I know what will happen to me? The stage is already set, though. An evolutionary psychobiologist is quoted in the book *After The Death of a Child* by Ann Finkbeiner. "When mammals opted for a family way of life, they set the stage for one of the most distressful forms of human suffering."

It's true. Our pain is created by those we love, involuntarily or voluntarily. Parents who lose a child to suicide, violence, or a senseless accident live with constant anguish. Resolution is not possible. And when your child dies from disease, as Sean did, it is never fully resolved either. There are some things I will never come to terms with: sins of commission, sins of omission. I didn't do everything I should have for Sean, and now I have to grow accustomed to living with tension, to knowing that things are not quite right and never will be.

I am living for the surviving members of my family right now, and I try not to think about the future because it stretches out with unbearable emptiness. When Hayley is raised and leaves home, what can I possibly find of meaning in my life? But again, I cannot predict how I will feel in ten years. Perhaps at some point in time, life will feel different than it does now.

SEAN

I have been at my mother's house for the past few days, where Mary and her children are visiting. I drove back to Twin Falls today, because I wanted to put flowers on Sean's grave and be home on the anniversary of his death. I need to be away from the bustle of family activities, removed from the laughter and cheer. It has been wonderful for Tyler and Hayley to be with their cousins, but it is a mixed bag for me. I love being with my sister, of course, because I can talk to her about anything and she understands, but Sean was not there. His death has left a vast, empty space, and the cousins nearest his age felt it deeply. On three or four nights I cried myself to sleep. Angels don't comfort me as they did in the past. Maybe I don't want them to.

We have put a few of Sean's things in a decorated box: the eye patch he wore the final month of his life, his sunglasses, an Indiana Jones T–shirt, Michigan State basketball shorts, and his silk boxers. His athletic trophies are in the box as well, wrapped in a Harley Davidson shirt that reads *"Legends live where legends roam."* I have also saved the letters and cards he received from people during his illness. Eventually, I want to have a wooden chest made with his name carved on the lid, like Beth's in *Little Women*, so I can store in one place all the things that defined Sean and what his life meant, including his baseball caps, photos, and scrapbook.

Photographs of Sean are displayed all over the house, intermingled with an equal number of Tyler and Hayley. I am not hiding Sean's pictures, pretending that he was never here. He is a significant part of our life. He is still our son, and Hayley's and Tyler's brother. How can we erase his existence? I refuse to. Call it a shrine if you like.

During Sean's illness, I remember thinking that if I had known this was going to happen, I would not have had children. I have changed my mind. The family experience is meaningful and life enriching. I would do it again, many times over. Sean has literally changed my life, and I cannot explain how. Although I think of my future as an empty space, it would have been desolate if I hadn't known Sean for 14 years. He was a gift from a benevolent God, from a loving universe, given not to punish us by taking him prematurely, but to make our lives fuller. Now he has returned to his real home, and it is not here with us.

There were no grandiose, obvious miracles. Sean was not miraculously healed. There was no spontaneous remission. In spite of all our efforts and prayers, he died anyway. But perhaps the real miracle was that the family survived. Al and I are still Sean's parents, and more committed to each other than ever before. Maybe we need to search a little deeper for our own miracles, and learn to accept that they are usually not the ones we ask for.

I don't feel bitter towards God. He didn't single me out, and Sean was not being punished when he died. Perhaps he was being rewarded, or maybe his death was simply one event in the natural order of things. I don't know. As for myself, I did get something out of all this pain. I know what real love is now. I learned about it from the child with no hair, a fragile body, pale skin, and an uncertain future.

I had another dream about Sean the other night, after months of waiting. He was walking down a long, straight road, all alone. I discovered that Al had let him go, and I was upset. I jumped into the car and raced down the road, trying to catch up with Sean before it was too late, but by the time I found him, he had already arrived at his destination. I got out of the car, and he walked towards me. "I love you, Sean," I offered desperately.

He smiled and said, "I know that."

SEAN

I dreamed about him last night as well. In the dream, Hayley was sleeping in our bedroom on the main level of our house, so she was accounted for, but Sean was not. I was climbing the stairs looking for him, and somehow I could visualize Tyler, who is away at school most of the time, hidden behind the closed door to his bedroom. I knew he was accounted for, but I could not find Sean, and I didn't know what to do.

"How will I find him?" I asked myself in a panic. Where had he gone, and what was I going to do if he didn't return? Was he lost? When I reached the top of the stairway, Sean suddenly appeared. He was smiling sweetly, like he had a wonderful secret, and he reached out his arms for me. We embraced, and I felt his flat chest (there were no bulky broviac tubes) tight against my own.

Sean has tried so hard to let me know he is still around, and that there is no death, just a separation. I am afraid, though, that I will never see my lost child again in this life, not in the harsh light of day, not with my one-dimensional eyes. I cannot hear him say, "Good night, Mom. I love you," and I can no longer touch his velvety cheek or rub the back of his bald head.

But if I can see and feel him in my dreams every once in a while, maybe he's not really lost. Maybe I am the one who is lost on this planet called Earth. I hope some day Sean will find me.

He will always be our beautiful boy.

"Sean was here—"

There is no end.
For the soul there is never birth nor death.
Nor, having once been, does it ever cease to be.
It is unborn, eternal, ever-existing,
undying and primeval.

The Bhagavad-Gita

SEAN

SEAN

READING LIST

Beattie, Melody. *The Lessons of Love.* Harper San Francisco, 1994.

Buscaglia, Ph.D., Leo. *The Fall of Freddie the Leaf: A Story of Life for All Ages.* Slack Incorporated, 1982.

Davidson, Joyce D., Doka, Kenneth J., editors. *Living With Grief,* Hospice Foundation of America, 1998.

Eadie, Betty J. *Embraced By The Light*, Gold Leaf Press, 1992.

Finkbeiner, Ann K. *After the Death Of A Child: Living With Loss Through The Years*, The Free Press, 1996.

Gibran, Kahlil. *The Prophet,* Alfred A. Knopf, 1923.

Gunther, John. *Death Be Not Proud,* HarperCollins Publishers, 1949.

Kubler–Ross, M.D., Elisabeth. *On Children and Death,* Simon and Schuster, 1983.

Kubler–Ross, M.D., Elisabeth. *The Wheel of Life: A Memoir of Living and Dying,* Scribner, 1997.

Kubler–Ross, M.D., Elisabeth. *The Tunnel And The Light,* Marlowe and Company, 1999.

Moody, M.D., Raymond Jr. *The Light Beyond,* Bantam Books, 1988.

Morse, M.D., Melvin. *Closer To The Light: Learning From The Near-Death Experiences of Children,* Ivy Books, 1990.

Morse, M.D., Melvin. *Parting Visions,* Harper Collins Publishers, 1994.

Morse, M.D., Melvin. *Transformed By The Light,* Ivy Books, 1992.

O'Reilly, Sean, James, and Tim, editors. *The Road Within: True Stories of Transformation and the Soul,* Travelers' Tales Inc., 1997.

Oyler, Chris; with Beth Polson and Laurie Becklund. *Go Toward The Light,* Harper and Row Publishers, 1988.

Pearson, Carol Lynn. *Beginnings,* Doubleday & Company, 1967.

Rosof, Barbara D. *The Worst Loss: How Families Heal From The Death Of A Child*, Henry Holt and Company, 1994.

Vest, Joe, edited by. *The Open Road: Walt Whitman on Death and Dying,* Four Corners Editions, 1996.